# ALPINE ARCHAEOLOGY

## PATRICK HUNT

ARIEL BOOKS
NEW YORK

**Patrick Hunt** is on the Classics and Archaeology faculty at Stanford University, where he has been Director of the Stanford Alpine Archaeology Project since 1994.

His Hannibal research is sponsored by the National Geographic Society, with a grant from their Expedition Council for 2007-2008. He is also an elected Fellow of the Royal Geographic Society (London) for montane exploration and has served as President of the Stanford Society of the Archaeological Institute of America (since 1995).

His archaeology research has also been featured on the HISTORY CHANNEL broadcasts on various topics and in ARCHAEOLOGY Magazine (Jan/Feb 2007). Author of many global archaeology journal articles, his archaeology books include TEN DISCOVERIES THAT REWROTE HISTORY (Fall 2007) from Penguin/Plume and other monographs.

Hunt's Ph.D. (1991) is in Archaeology from the Institute of Archaeology, UCL, University of London.


Published 2007
11 10 09 08 07     1 2 3 4 5
Printed in the United States of America
ISBN: 1-934-26900-X (paper)
978-1-9342690-0-8 (paper)

**UNIVERSITY READERS**
San Diego 92121
800-200-3908
info@universityreaders.com
www.universityreaders.com

# CONTENTS

# ACKNOWLEDGMENTS

This book is the fruit of more than a decade of labor, not that it took so long to write but rather that its observations were made over time in numerous field seasons and gradually built up over years of research in the Alps. This book is not intended to be comprehensive, but rather is a small picture of our work to date. Its archaeological relevance (as a work in progress) to other Alpine contexts is more to be inferred from common elements than expressly stated here. The first part of the book is derived from our fieldwork, mostly in the Grand-St-Bernard region, and the second part derives from our ongoing research attempting to trace Hannibal's route across the Alps.

Many students assisted in the patient collection of data and nearly all those students between 1994-2006 hiked and climbed over Alpine mountains and down into Alpine valleys searching for often elusive archaeological remains or tracking Hannibal across the mountains. Sometimes we marveled together peering down at the courage of the tiniest brilliant flowers growing in sheltered cracks in rocks, sometimes on our hands and knees we exulted over the finds of thumbprints of potters pressed into potsherds still surviving after thousands of years or over glass, or while holding up just-excavated bronze and even silver coins minted by Romans and then buried for millennia far from their points of origin. Sometimes on our backs we were awed by meteor showers in night skies filled with stars. It was worth it when with tired hands and feet we finished a day's research and then found a season's satisfaction under craggy peaks that were there long before we came and will still be there long after we are gone. So this is those students' book as well. This book is dedicated to at least a generation of wonderful students for whom the Alps will always evoke shared memories of spectacular vistas and camaraderie.

There is also one individual to whom this book is dedicated. Robert Tousey, whose vision and big heart are unforgettable, worked for years on my photographs and gradually brought my teaching via archaic slide projectors to digital and computer projection and into the 21<sup>st</sup> century. Bob was in many ways my mentor and teacher in matters archaeological and pedagogical.

Generous sponsors have encouraged and underwritten our Stanford Alpine Archaeology Project by providing the resources to dream and study all these years in the Alps. These benefactors include Peter and Helen Bing, Herant and Stina Katchadourian and Cordell and Susan Hull, to all of whom I owe a great debt. Gratitude is also expressed to the Classics Department at Stanford University and to its Chairman, Professor Richard Martin, who has always encouraged scholarship by his own example. Friends and encouragers who have followed this research from the outset include Fritz and Beverly Maytag. Last but not least, I am grateful for the sponsorship of the National Geographic Society through a major grant from the Expedition Council for our Hannibal research in 2007-2008.

# ILLUSTRATIONS

# Chapter One

# WHY ALPINE ARCHAEOLOGY?

## Introduction

Why should alpine archaeology deserve a separate category? One does not usually hear or read about desert archaeology or tropical archaeology as separate sub-disciplines within the larger study of general archaeology, yet each unique environment presents different problems, advantages and disadvantages. The study of alpine archaeology as a separate sub-discipline presents unique contextual and climatic circumstances that play a large role in both the location and preservation of artifactual material.

That there should be some focus within archaeology specifically oriented to mountains and the Alps in particular is not surprising when the global picture is examined. Virtually 11% of the Earth's land surface is higher than 2,000 meters (6400 ft) or above a mile in elevation.[1] This altitude, while modifying human interaction, has hardly prohibited human occupation or even long-term presence.

The working definition of alpine archaeology relevant to this text is of that specific montane or high altitude archaeology pertaining to the European cultures or material remains and types across the convex mountain arc of the Alps in France, Switzerland, Austria, Germany and what was Yugoslavia but is now Slovenia. [2] This text does not generally consider or report on archaeology from other global high montane elevations on different continents, even though many of the same considerations are applicable, for example, in the Rocky Mountains in continental North America or the Caucasus mountains in Asia, etc.

The primary archaeology considered in this text concentrates on contexts in montane elevations above 800 meters (approximately 2700 ft. altitude) or the alpine valleys between these mountains where the general prevailing climate is dictated by the mountains above.

The upper elevation limits for alpine archaeology could go as high as the Alps themselves – including Mont Blanc at 4807 meters (15,771 ft.) – but significant human presence has traditionally been clustered below the fluctuating yet near-permanent historical snowline around 3600 meters (11,520 ft.) in summer.

The chronology involved is generally different and often later than in other locales, generally beginning from the Stone Age, generally Mesolithic, circa 12,000 - 9,000 years BP (10,000-7,000 BCE), Neolithic circa 9,000 - 6,000 years BP (7,000-4,000 BCE), Copper Age circa 6,000 – 4,000 BP (4,000 – 2,000 BCE),[3] Bronze Age circa 4,000 – 2800 BP (2,000 – 800 BCE), Iron Age circa 2,800 – 2,200 BP (800 – 200 BCE) from Hallstatt to La Tène cultures, Roman and Gallo-Roman circa 2,200 - 1,500 BP (200 BCE – 500 CE), Medieval circa 1500- 500 BP (500 – 1500 CE).

Mesolithic archaeology in the Alps is usually a reliable *terminus post quem* (Latin for "point after which…") because heavy glaciation in the Alps prior to this period appears to have obliterated anything earlier as the underlying glacial moraine acted like a huge blotter grinding away the earth's surface as glaciers wiped it clean like a slow-moving blotter of ice and rock.

Thus, Paleolithic archaeological material is almost nonexistent in this glacially dominated alpine landscape prior to 10,000 BCE, looking then much like the topography around the Schreckhorn at 4078 meters or around 13,000 ft. (Figure 1) above Grindelwald with adjacent glaciers in the Bernese Oberland.

**1. ALPINE SCHRECKHORN**

This researcher has spent the past several decades concentrating on montane or alpine archaeology in the Alps themselves but also in other montane zones where certain contextual circumstances may overlap. The Andes mountains of South America, the Apennine range of Italy, the Lebanon – Mt. Hermon massif of the Levant, the Tuxtlas and Sierra Madre ranges of Central America (Mexico), the Sierra Nevada and Pacific Coast ranges of the U.S. among others, are some of the contexts where this researcher has spent time in archaeological study from which some principles are drawn for this text.

Biogeography and geomorphology are themselves important for all archaeologists who wish to draw greater inferences from their fieldwork about the larger questions that human prehistory and history have followed without necessarily having any conscious attention for having done so. If, as this author has stated for years, geomorphology shapes history and humans live by the adaptive constraints of biogeography [4] (note how most human population for millennia have been concentrated in the mid latitude temperate climate zone and fairly close to large water masses and coastal areas or river outlets at low altitude), then human occupation in the Alps is somewhat anomalous.

### Types of Global Climatic Environments

As mentioned, the types of environments in which archaeological and cultural materials are found include *tropical, desert, temperate, alpine* or *montane, and Arctic* (or *Antarctic*). Some of these environments are dependent on latitude, others on prevailing winds and geomorphology, among other factors. That human prehistory and history have been much influenced by climate needs no elaborate proof, yet because Alpine prehistory and history have been so strongly determined by paleoclimates [5] for the past ±10,000 years, [6] it is important to differentiate some major climatic zones. To best understand alpine climate in context, it is also necessary to briefly discuss other climates.

### Tropical

Tropical is further defined by the quantity of liquid moisture, either by high precipitation in this wettest of biomes (minimum 60 inches but may exceed 160 inches, in any case usually above 1000 mm per year) [7] or high relative humidity (above 50%) along with a higher year-round median temperature (above 25 ° C / 75 ° F (usually between 68-82 ° F) and a near absence of seasons (although there may be both wet/dry seasons without much transition). The total number of species in tropics may be up to

35-40 per hectare and this biome may produce 0.2-0.7 lbs per square foot of biomass per year.[8]  Of these climatic zones, tropical is generally found within 30 ° north or south latitude from the equator, and Arctic and Antarctic zones generally found above 60 ° north or south latitude from the equator. Therefore, tropics are generally fixed climatic zones.

*Desert*

On the other hand, although often contiguous with temperate and even subtropical or even tropical latitudes, desert – defined mostly by high aridity (under 15-35 mm or 4-10 inches of precipitation), very low relative humidity (under 18%) and often fairly high daily temperature (median above 30 ° C / 85 ° F) can be found anywhere moisture from prevailing winds is either blocked by mountains or already been released in those mountains where little rain shadow exists. For example, the deserts of Egypt can be well within the tropical latitudes north, as can some of the Peruvian coastal desert around 13 ° latitude south, but in both cases moisture from large evaporitic bodies of water like oceans has already long been lost.  When wind-driven moisture from a body of water hits mountain ranges, the air is forced up and upon cooling reaches dew point and releases its water rather than carry it across a plain. This is called *orographic* (montane-determined) precipitation. With a prevailing westerly wind (form the west), because the Sierra Nevada range on the U.S. Pacific coast blocks and drains this moisture from reaching points eastward, the eastern Nevada side of this high plain is desertified. The same phenomenon works in reverse in South America where the easterly winds (from the east) are blocked by the very high Andes mountains even in the tropics, thus resulting in the huge water-rich Amazon basin on the tropical eastern side and the deserts on the western side of the Andes, even though tropical in latitude. At the other extreme to tropics, biomass productivity in deserts is very limited, usually under 0.06 lbs per square foot per year. [9]

*Temperate*

The other climatic zone, primary and most important to archaeology in terms of concentration of artifacts buried, is actually the temperate climate areas between 30 ° – 60 ° latitudes north and south. Not surprisingly, this temperate zone is where most of the world's population has been historically concentrated. This temperate climate zone has been relatively stable in the past with precipitation, temperature and humidity within the high and low extremes of tropics and deserts but with distinct seasons. Temperate climate biomass of 6 lbs per square foot has a productivity range around 0.1-0.5 lbs per year.[10]   Unfortunately, the actual preservation of artifactual material in the temperate climate zone is generally not as good as might be found in both desert and arctic climatic zones, for reasons explained shortly.

Temperate climates always have the highest density of human modification in terms of artifacts *buried*, as mentioned, due to prehistoric and historic demographics of where people  have usually lived, but they do not retain the highest density of artifacts *preserved*. Variations occur between the cold and wet state versus the warm and dry state fluctuations so prevalent in temperate climates. Wet states increase solubility of materials, since water is the universal solvent, accelerating the loss of structural integrity. Dry states also contribute to the problem with the evacuation of water  – carrying away matter through leaching - via the process of slaking. This is also a function of lost structural integrity due to the differential of thermal contraction and expansion.

*Arctic / Antarctic*

Arctic and Antarctic climatic zones above 60 ° latitude north and south can be excellent for material preservation because of annual average low temperature (under 2 ° C or around 35 ° F) and a natural almost permanent frozen state except in some tundra contexts. Yet, Arctic and Antarctic can actually be similar to "desert" conditions if the water is thereby inaccessible for solubility in its frozen state rather than liquid state.

Because of low temperature and short growing season, biomass productivity in tundra (polar desert) is low, ranging between 0.02-0.08 lbs per square foot per year. [11]

**2. ALPINE MAP**

*Alpine*

By the above definition applicable here, the alpine zone usually lies within the temperate zone in terms of latitude - completely so in the European Alps (see Alpine Map, Figure 2) – but at higher elevation where the climate can mimic Arctic or Antarctic conditions for at least half the year. The old geographer's adage that "altitude mirrors or parallels latitude" in terms of climatic expectations is certainly true in the Alps. Above 3000 m (10,000 ft.) elevation the general climatic zone is closest to arctic or above 60 ° latitude. Below 3000 m elevation but above 2000 m, the climatic zones gradations often approximate the same conditions found normally between 50 – 60 ° latitude, and can result in a frozen state of snow and ice for nine months per year. Yet, alpine summers at 2400 m (8000 ft.) elevation can be relatively mild and even warmish with temperatures up to 19 ° C (around 66 ° F) after spring snowmelt, although alpine summers at this elevation are generally so variable that it can snow almost any day of summer in the right cold temperature conditions. After spring thaw, the resulting short but intense period of vegetative growth and the higher likelihood of rain rather than snow makes the alpine climate excellent for material preservation except during the summer months. This will be elaborated shortly.

Another working definition of Alpine climate – not necessarily applicable here because it is not specifically about climates of the Alps but mountain climates in general – explains it differently. A term called dry adiabatic lapse rate suggests that the rate of change results in a decrease of 10°C per each kilometer of increased altitude. This results in that if one walks 100 meters (roughly 320 ft.) up a mountain, the difference is about equal to walking 80 kilometers (45' or 0.75° of latitude) towards the North Pole ("altitude mirrors latitude"). The best theorists about cold climate relevant to this discussion are most likely Koppen and Nordenskiold. [12]

Some interesting climatic variations exist in places, for example, like the high Andes Mountains in South America or other specific mountain peaks within the tropical latitudes like Mt. Kilimanjaro (5892 meters or 19,331 ft) in Africa. The tree line in the Alps averages around 6,550 ft whereas in the Himalayas it is closer to 11,150 feet, mostly due to the higher latitude of the Alps.[13] In tropical montane contexts, the snowline is much higher and prevailing climate may mimic temperate zones at lower latitudes but here at much higher altitudes. Where in higher latitudes boreal taiga coniferous forest may cover thousands of hectares or square miles across a continent above 50-55 ° latitude even at low altitude, in the Andes and in Africa such coniferous forests are not only rare but are instead replaced by hardwoods at 3000 meters (9,600 ft.) and scrub forest thriving even at 4000 meters (12,800 ft.) and the snowline may instead be above 5000 meters (16,000 ft). In such unique contexts, the "latitude parallels altitude" assumption does not apply and other biological anomalies exist such as hummingbirds with wingspreads of almost 20 cm and avocado fruit growing to be almost as large as soccer balls at 10,000 ft. because the altitude is mitigated by tropical latitude.

Naturally, there are many other global locations where the climatic zoning is transitional or anomalies apply that may hybridize or alter the normal climatic patterns or expectations. The Alps also have internal climatic variations depending, for example, on whether the prevailing influence is from the cooler northern European plain, since most northern alpine weather is determined by the westerly winds that can also cool from the north in their Coriolis effect driven gyres, just as most southern alpine weather can be influenced by the warmer Mediterranean to the south. Even those contexts on the European continental divide can exhibit fluctuations where both climatic influences can alternate.

Climate variation within the Alps from north to south and west to east is due to a complex set of interrelated and multivariate factors – including the great temperature fluctuations and water cycle (including snow pack and snow release) within the year from winter to summer (unlike the Arctic) - that greatly affect vegetation and overall phytomass.[14] Partly dependent on this interannual climatic variation within a yearly cycle, also understanding the microclimates in deep alpine valleys between high massifs must factor into the equation the geomorphological and climatic differences between mostly east-west Alps regions such as the Bernese Oberland and Pennine Alps vs. the north-south Alps regions, e.g. the Cottian, Tarentaise, Alpes Maritimes, and yet others such as the Mont Blanc massif that have combined features of both north-south and west-east. These variables help to make Alpine climatology a very complex subject, one where climatic generalizations – and even visible changes like tree lines at one location and elevation – are often suspect and difficult topics, especially where sheer rock may otherwise bar vegetation from a natural biome.

Global warming poses another problem for making long-term Alpine climate assumptions, with expected glacial regression to lose more than 50% of its cover since 1850 by 2025 at present rates of loss.[15] Such loss of huge, solar reflective and cooling ice cover may result in enormous temperature and vegetation changes in the Alps, such that all previous assumptions about Alpine climate since prehistory may no longer apply. Mesoscale Alpine Climate that uses a prior century of meteorological data as a benchmark from which to quantify predictable weather patterning is currently engaged in a systematic re-evaluation of Alpine climate, having also to consider prior data no longer valid. [16] Factoring in the fast-changing range of twentieth century data against more stable varve and dendrochronology dating of Alpine contexts since 1600 suggest that current calibration models for understanding Alpine climate make the quantification of Alpine meteorology less stable than is desired.[17] The well-recorded twentieth century alone is inadequate to read as a template for past Alpine climate. [18] All this new questioning makes it difficult to estimate the long-term climatic stability of the Alps in the future as a reliable gauge relative to the assumptions about Alpine climate since prehistory as recorded in varves, glacial ice and tree rings.


*The Agents Working Against Material Preservation: Water, Heat, Light*

Survival of archaeological materials is usually dependent on several factors, perhaps the most important being the exposure to *water, heat* and *light*, all three of which will contribute to or accelerate the destruction of artifacts – especially organic material – in sufficient concentration. Too much water ("the universal solvent") causes hydrolysis or solubility, which breaks down material, too much light causes photolysis which bleaches out pigments, and too much heat increases electron mobility.

*Deserts*, being arid, lack water and can therefore assist the material preservation of some materials, although too much light and heat can cause problems for certain artifacts, causing them to become brittle when they lose all moisture. On the other hand, the deserts of ancient Egypt in places like Oxyrhynchus have preserved the trash-piles of discarded papyrus, textiles and even leather sandals.

*Arctic* or extreme cold temperature environments create a near-cryogenic state where organic artifacts are sometimes almost perfectly preserved in a frozen refrigerated state where the same water content in liquid form could eventually dissolve the same tissues ice preserves. Ice crystals, however, can cause tissue swelling and rupturing since water in the solid state expands.

*Temperate* regions suffer from seasonal fluctuations in the abundance of all water, light and heat in both good and bad circumstances (spring and fall as seasons are not good for artifacts in a rainy climate because artifacts decompose at a faster rate; summer and winter are better if dryness and coldness contribute to artifact survival).

*Tropics* generally create the worst of all possible circumstances for artifact survival – especially organic – because there is most often a simultaneous abundance of all three agents of change (water, heat, light). High rainfall of a higher temperature such as warm rain wreaks havoc with materials. Excessive light in relatively high humidity also accelerates decomposition unless a vegetation canopy protects vulnerable artifacts. Even certain stone artifacts of a higher solubility rate (such as limestone) can be significantly impacted in tropical climates. Maya carved reliefs of soft limestone such as in an interior courtyard of the so-called "Governor's Palace" at Palenque, for example, are eroding quickly as jungle canopy is removed.[19] Then these reliefs bear the brunt of wet / dry slaking states with the coefficient of thermal expansion and contraction at its most polarizing effects.

*Alpine* regions of Europe – defined mostly by altitude here – can provide optimum environments for artifact survival between half to three quarters of a year when ice and snow cover the artifacts or where cold soil prevails. Because alpine temperature is rarely hot, and because cold inhibits diffusion and the resulting oxidation of materials, alpine contexts are mildly benign relative to tropical contexts. The spectacular "Ötzi" the Ice Man find in 1991, from around 5,300 years old in the alpine Neolithic age, was well preserved in a near glacier until glacial regression and massive snowmelt and ice loss over time (assumed to be the second half of the 20th century) exposed his body at around 3,300 meters elevation (a little below 11,000 ft.).[20] Artifacts associated with the Ice Man included stone tools but also preserved textiles (skins and leathers) in clothes and quivers and even preserved wood handles of weapons and tools. Inorganic artifacts also are often better preserved as well in Alpine contexts. Oxides of certain metals (iron, copper, silver, tin, lead, etc,) or their alloys are often reduced in Alpine contexts, so that corrosion products can be limited in the amount of rust, patina or other oxide accumulating from material degradation.

*Shared Features with other Archaeological Environments*

Like other types of archaeological inquiry in almost any conceivable global context (including nautical) involving field excavation, Alpine archaeology also requires a sequence of processes and common applications including survey and laying out a grid based on benchmarks, data points, an understanding of stratigraphy, some form of sieving and finds processing as well as recording with sample tags and some type of imaging (computer, digital, video or other photographic instruments). These are just a few of the more obvious shared features in fieldwork methods.

Other shared features with all archaeology include separation and careful study of artifactual materials (including provenance and conservation research) and the utilization of specialists in a diverse range of sub-disciplines, including but not limited to ceramic technology, archaeometallurgy, numismatics, bioarchaeology, soil chemistry, architecture, geology and geomorphology and many more facets of archaeological research.

## Unique Features of Alpine Archaeology

Alpine field archaeology is also somewhat different than many types of field archaeology in that its locus is generally at a higher elevation. This may create breathing difficulties and it is usually much colder, which together can tax the energy of the individuals of a team more than usual at lower elevations. Inclement weather can also be much less predictable in that weather patterns can shift very quickly.

At elevations above 2400 meters (8000 ft.), it can snow any day of the year including high summer and nocturnal temperatures can easily drop below freezing. With these and other challenges of higher elevation than normal (if people usually live closer to sea level), it is often best not to extend field time in Alpine archaeology contexts for more than about three weeks at a time. After three weeks, our experience has been that the body's resistance begins to be challenged and that many of the team can become sick.

In addition to this fieldwork obstacle, other problems in applying normal methodology require some different practices, such as in sieving. Because the ground moisture in the Alps is generally higher due to regular intermittent rainfall (usually at least once a week) and because the drainage is also different because there is usually a much thinner layer of soil above bedrock, the soil can be fairly saturated with moisture, especially if there is insufficient sunlight with necessary ambient heat to evaporate it.

Thus, it is not expected that dry sieving will be the most successful, but rather that wet sieving will be more practical. On the other hand, an added challenge is that wet sieving must preserve the soil, which must be replaced on backfilling at the end of excavation and turf replaced because it can grow so slowly in short summer seasons. Just as tropics can be reduced to two seasons, wet and dry, so Alpine climate can result in only two seasons: spring (relative to lower elevations and temperate climates) and winter.

*Soil differences*

Another interesting feature of Alpine archaeology derives from soil types (pedology being the analytical science of soils). As stated, because there is more erosional stone (geological) than decaying vegetative material (biological) in high montane contexts, and because the thin alpine soils overlay bedrock, it behooves Alpine archaeologists to understand geological processes as well as oxidation processes. When montane soil is actually mostly glacial moraine, this can predetermine what vegetation can grow and thrive in it.

By contrast, alluvial soils in river plains are often deep and also rich in organic components from vegetative decay, so there can be a fairly rich biological component in alluvial soil. Depending on how deep a soil sample derives, a more even mix of organic (biological) to inorganic (geological) soil can be found.

A simple suggestion is that usually the more shallower one is looking on the soil column in any one place, the more organic the sources, and the deeper one is looking on the same soil column, the more inorganic the sources.

Deeper alluvial soils are often more complex than thin montane rock-derived soils, although even thin soil derived from glacial moraine can also be complexly heterogeneous. Alpine soil made up of quartz-rich eroded rock usually has a more acidic pH (below 7.0)), conversely montane soil made up of carbonate-rich eroded rock usually has a more alkali pH (above 7.0). Again, soil pH is as often determined by vegetation, for example where accumulated conifer needles create their own environment, as determining vegetation, for example when vegetation can only thrive in a certain pH range from the underlying geological stratum.

In addition, lower alpine soils under conifer forest cover are often podzolic with increased acidity from the conifer needles. Soil pH is covered in detail in Chapter Three.

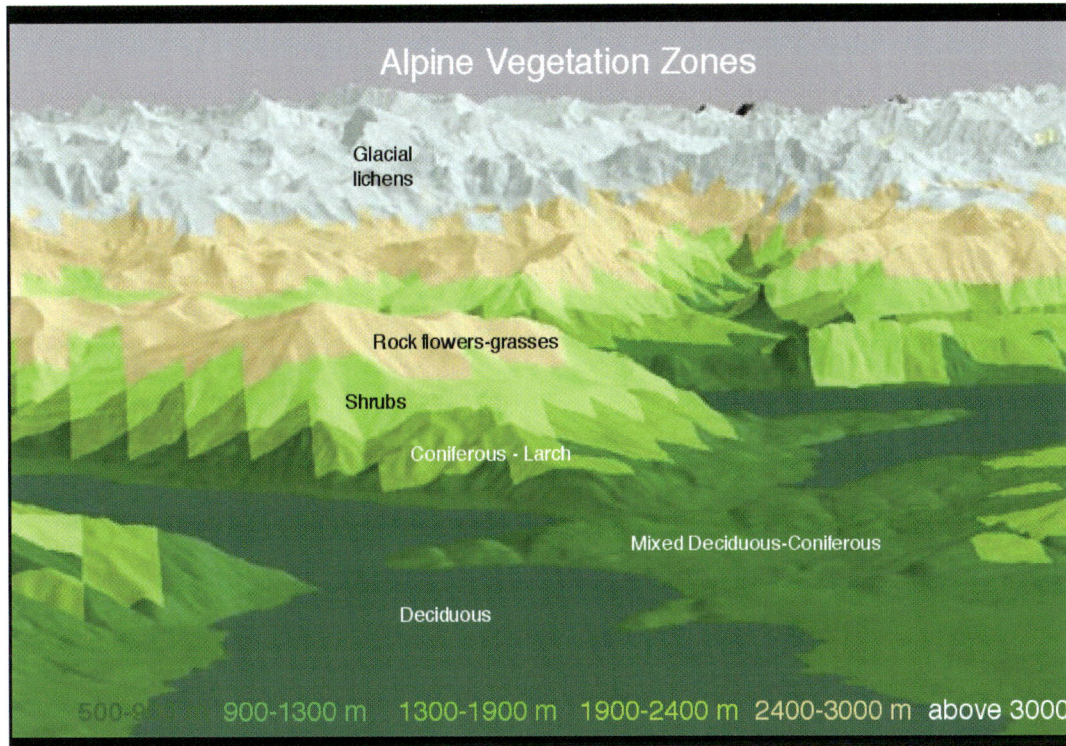

**Alpine Vegetation Zones**

Glacial lichens

Rock flowers-grasses

Shrubs

Coniferous - Larch

Mixed Deciduous-Coniferous

Deciduous

500-9... | 900-1300 m | 1300-1900 m | 1900-2400 m | 2400-3000 m | above 3000

**3. ALPINE VEGETATION ZONES**

*Vegetation Zones*

Vegetation zones encountered in the Alps are usually as follows: deciduous trees are found up to 700 meters elevation, then mixed deciduous and coniferous from about 700-1300 meters (around 2400-4000 ft.) elevation, mostly coniferous from 1300-1900 meters (around 4000-6000 ft.) elevation with a conifer tree line often around 1900 meters (around 6000 ft.) depending on which side of the Alps (Mediterranean side is warmer with a slightly higher tree line), shrub and scrub plants from 1900-2400 meters (around

7000-8000 ft.), alpine meadow flowers from 2400-3000 meters (roughly 8000-10,000 ft.) and mostly rockbound lichens above 3000 meters (roughly 10,000 ft.).

For archaeological purposes, lichenology itself can be useful in the Alps in positing generalized lichen growth rates relative to anthropogenic change of rock surfaces by human modification, such as carving routes through bedrock in steep, narrow places for greater ease of passages, but first the rate of growth of specific lichen colonies must be determined, since there is not necessarily a uniform rate over a region due to microcontext / microclimates, as we have noted in the Grand-St-Bernard where overall harsh weather dominates yearround, but a windswept area can be significantly different than a protected area a few meters away in terms of lichen growth. Other dating information about climatic change and the human record in the Alps can be inferred from dendrochronology (tree ring dating), particularly when wood like oak is used in human contexts and then preserved by the cold climate. While glacial varves (annual sediment deposits) are also useful for dating high altitude still lake climatic fluctuations, they are generally not as applicable to anthropogenic change unless they also contain human-derived carbonized wood ash and/or other aeolian particles or even ancient and modern pollutants.

The possibility of anthropogenic change and such realities as ancient deforestation must be considered, as it is likely that the ancient Alpine tree line in the Gallo-Roman period (200 BCE - 500 CE) might have been considerably higher given the normative logging and farming in almost continual practice since that time. On the other hand, tree line – not an exact altitude-derived Alpine phenomenon anyway - is much more difficult to predict, being based on many factors and is also dependent in paleoclimatic terms on whether the annual temperatures were higher or lower in antiquity, since a colder temperature could result in a lower tree line where trees would not have an optimum environment just as a warmer annual temperature could result in a higher tree line, although this is also on the type of timber in question with regard to its habitat. Reconstruction of alpine vegetation over a long historical period can be a very complicated matter. Anthropogenic change has also been a considerable factor in

16

the Alpine tree line in the historic period since the Bronze Age (post-2000 BCE). A schematicized version of a"typical" Alpine vegetation zoning is shown here (Figure 3), where the zigzags between 1300-1900 meters are quite often human-induced.

*Conclusion*

All these factors discussed here (climate, latitude, geological or biological soil sources, soil pH, soil depth, air temperature, humidity, amount and state of water in liquid (highly solvent) versus frozen (low diffusion and therefore not solvent) form, soil temperature, soil vegetation cover, altitude, etc.) each have a bearing on the complex equation as variables for preservation of archaeological artifacts in alpine contexts.

Alpine archaeology is therefore a sub-discipline of general archaeology, where it is important to understand and apply both common as well as unique features of field research to excavation and conservation of artifacts found in alpine contexts at higher elevations.

# Chapter Two

## ALPINE CLIMATE AND ITS EFFECTS ON ARCHAEOLOGY

### Introduction

How do altitude and its attendant climatic results affect archaeology? More to the point, how has the alpine climate affected human prehistory and history for the past 18,000 years since the Last Glacial Maximum? One easy answer is that while glaciers covered much of Europe around 18,000 years ago, the Alps themselves were hardly accessible until around 10-9,000 years beginning with the Mesolithic hunters who traversed these mountains again that had been hitherto an ice desert for the almost 10,000 prior years. [21]

Few realize that at the terminus of the last great glacial about 10,000 years ago (10,000 BP), "twice as many species of animals and plants became extinct as at any previous period of glacial advance and retreat." [22] This mass extinction of *megafauna* (large animals like mammoths and mastodons), itself climate-related, must have also greatly impacted human hunting patterns and diet in Europe. Mesolithic hunters in the Alps had multiple incentives for penetrating the mountains: not only were there still some biomes of animals important to their way of life as a huge source of biomass, but their known stone tool resources were also often derived from these same mountains. As glacial recession continues at a great pace, more stone scatter sites from Mesolithic tool making are found under receding glaciers that were at a recent maximum in the early 19th century, and prehistoric butchery sites of animal herds are often found not far from these same tool making resource contexts.

Since 1994, the Stanford Alpine Archaeology Project has had an annual active learning experience about this relationship between alpine climate and archaeology.

Paleoclimatology, palynology and anthropogenic change over millennia are part of our annual field research. Our field observations are discussed in this chapter as well as throughout this book.

**4. ALPINE CLIMATE/SATELLITE PHOTO**

Some general data about Alpine climate is apropos. Not only is the European Alpine high altitude above 2200 meters a cold biome, but also above the deciduous larch (*Laryx sp.*) tree line usually between 1900-2600 meters, where summer temperatures range on average between -6 degrees Celsius to around 14 degrees Celsius. The average minimum precipitation in the Pennine Alps at 2200-2400 meters in the Grand-St-Bernard Pass is around 30 meters per year, at least 60% of which occurs as snow. Some years the precipitation exceeds 45 meters. Late summer and early fall satellite images as shown here (Figure 4) can easily show incoming storms building up from the west as the prevailing weather direction.

As mentioned earlier, another component that reflects climatic effects is Alpine vegetation. Global vegetation has been carefully classified for years, with the consensus often following the Raunkiaer classification developed in 1934, where Raunkiaer's axioms of climate observed that the plant biomes of the world generally respond to several stresses including low temperature and available water. Cold temperatures also make water scarce, so it is surprising to many travelers in the Alps that the coniferous larch tree biome so ubiquitous in the Alps, unlike so many other conifers, has responded in adapting to its dual stress of cold and low water availability (because the water is frozen) by becoming deciduous. This is just one interesting phenomenon that sets Alpine climate and vegetation apart from the arctic climate periphery of tundra scrub vegetation as well as set apart from taiga forests of the northernmost temperate climate zones.

Alpine growing season, primarily in early to late summer, is also determined by climate and latitude, among other factors, including the amount of sunlight for photosynthesis and temperature, as already mentioned. It should be no surprise that cloud cover is important here, as there is considerable variation in Alpine vegetation biosomes and overall phytomass depending on whether these are on the northern or southern flanks of the Alps in a convex arching east-west direction as well as eastern or western ranges in a north-south direction. The northern Alpine flanks are considerably colder than the Mediterranean flanks of the Alps because of increased cloud cover diffusing solar radiation and diminishing heat. Cloud cover must also be considered as prehistorically and historically important for archaeological purposes and the relative density of material remains expected in northern vs. southern Alps. [23]

The typical Alpine growing season above 2200 meters for shrubby plants (including mountain azalea and scrub juniper) is around 160 days. At night even summer temperatures often drop below freezing at elevations above 2200 meters. When warmer air masses from the Mediterranean in Italy meet the colder air masses of Northern Europe in Switzerland, a heavy fog often occurs around between 2200-2500 meters elevation with a thick cold air blanket in the passes between the continental divide where we work on the general border of the two countries. Within a few meters of each other in our site area, snow melt will flow either into the Mediterranean from the Po watershed or the Rhone watershed. The areas of alpine Switzerland (including the Grand-St-Bernard pass region) above 2200 meters have an annual median temperature not exceeding 5-7° C, essentially due to year round snow mass as a function of altitude.[24]

## *Field Challenges of Altitude and Climate*

"Going up a mountain is, in biological terms, rather like undertaking a much longer journey toward the poles: the changing vegetation types encountered with increasing altitude resemble the succession of biomes with increasing latitude. Mountains have a climate of their own and thus a distinctive flora and fauna, and add diversity to a region." [25]

This is just another way of stating, as mentioned in the previous chapter, the old adage that altitude mimics latitude. This is a possibly more obvious in the Alps than almost any other place I have conducted archaeological research, because it can snow any day of the year at 2472 meters (8200 ft elevation). Since 1994, part of our project has been conducted in the Grand-St-Bernard Pass, at the montane junction of the Mont Blanc Massif and the Pennine Alps on an international border where Switzerland, Italy meet (we are also about 30 miles as the eagle flies from the French border). Last year's summer fieldwork was interrupted, as usual, by a mid-July snowfall that would in principle be lovely in December but is often frustrating when the fieldwork window is already narrow. Each year we usually have to wait until the winter snow melts to begin excavating, otherwise if we chop through snow and ice we have only muck underneath. If we wait too long, however, by mid-August the autumn begins early and we meet increasing snowfall again. This means that each year - depending on uncontrollable and rarely predictable variables - we have to be watching long-term European meteorology while still planning a fairly set time to do our annual fieldwork between July and August and hope for the best. Permanent active web cams set up across Switzerland assist us in accessing immediate snowfall melt data and inclement weather conditions while we are still stateside via the Internet. The Swiss National Atlas image (Figure 5) showing blue and pink hues for temperature distinctions suggests an annual median temperature of 13-17 ° C for the lower pink values and a median around 5-7° C for the higher blue values, generally higher than 2000 meters (6400 ft) elevation and even lower median annual temperatures above 3000 meters.

I sometimes hear complaints from students during alpine fieldwork on cold days that we often may experience frostbite on our fingers, especially during prolonged wet sieving alongside or in glacial streams. For the most part, dry sieving is unusual here in the Alps, because the soil will never quite dry out under typical circumstances between

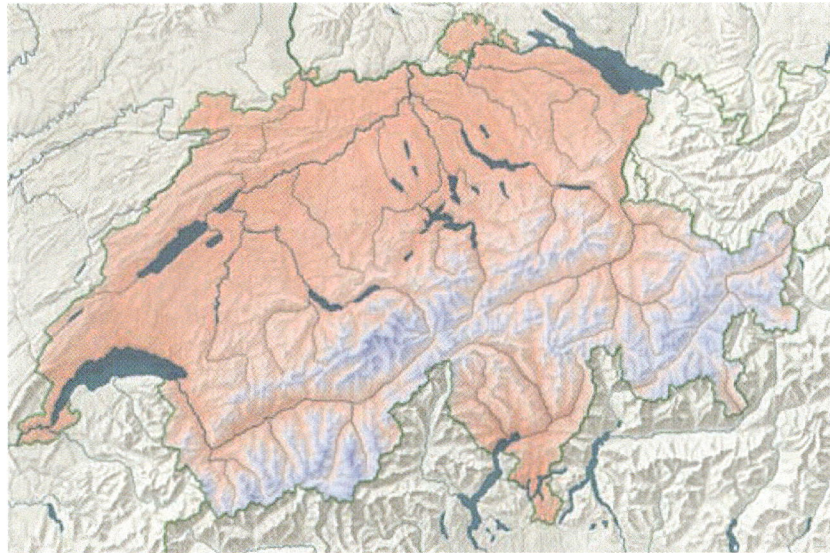

**5. ALPINE CLIMATE – TEMPERATURE MAP**

July and August if it is overcast for a week or so and or saturated soils spread out to be sieved must be covered with tarps during the frequent alpine showers. Even a cold wind helps a little to dry out wet soil whereas warm sunshine is often scarce. Because we have occasionally lost too much overburden topsoil by total wet sieving down at the nearest glacial melt runoff stream - with sieved soil too easily washed away - we sometimes have had difficulty in backfilling a season's site work (having to import rock and local schist gravel instead). Thus, now we always do double or treble sieving, first by spreading out wet soil to dry as much as possible before we do an intermediate "dry" sieve and then we conduct our final our wet sieving at the stream when most of the soil has already been removed onsite to be backfilled. This sieving system presents challenges but retains most of our topsoil, which we then replant with sod removed at the initial surface excavation. Another problem we face is the issue of stamina for weeks of fieldwork. After more than three weeks working above 2200 meters, we find decreasing productivity due to physical exhaustion, intermittent high altitude sleep deprivation and increasing general health malaise where common colds develop due to near-permanent wet shoes and general low temperatures with wind chill factors. This is true even for a healthy staff that is generally athletic and with an average age of around 20 years old.

Some of the field conditions, while frustrating for fieldwork, however, actually promote preservation of materials. While there is a lot of water in the region, it is in the frozen state for at least nine months a year. Inorganic materials like silver and bronze coins are often in pristine condition, with little to no need of conservation. The resulting low diffusion inhibits a great deal of metals corrosion. Bronze artifacts, for example, are often in excellent state of preservation and we have even found part of the wooden haft of a Roman spear preserved inside the bronze spearhead's shank sockle-receptacle.

### Metals and Glass Preservation

Bronze coins excavated in near mint condition include one from the Celtic Sequani tribe (cf. Henri de La Tour *Atlas de Monnaies Gauloises* # 5368)[26] with its horse image from the 2nd c. BCE [27] and the silvered bronze Hadrianic coin with traces of iron horning circa CE 135. Also in excellent condition was the Roman bronze bucket handle found intact with its soldered bronze rivet pins (sometimes also called a "papillon"). There is substantial evidence now from even the prehistoric Copper Age that occupation in the Alps was often highly influenced by its potential for mining operations. This is an important point to remember for anyone conducting Alpine Archaeology: relict metal artifacts from long-term mining have a fairly high abundance in the Alps in such locations as St-Veran in the Queyras of France, not the least of which is their initial density coupled with their good state of preservation due to low oxidation from low temperature diffusion.

Roman glass with the customary bubbles - including a circa 1st century CE green glass handle for a square glass bottle of likely Syrian origin - has 0% birefringent iridescence from devitrification (loss of silica) as is so commonly found in temperate zone climates even in marginally-aqueous contexts for Roman glass of this period. Also in perfect condition was the faience jewelry bead (turquoise-colored) with highest gloss showing no surface devitrification of its glaze.

The small silver coin hoard found in 2003 included datable coins from the late Republic and including mostly Augustan and Tiberian coins along with a famous M. Antoninus "Legionary Series" denarius circa 31 BCE - and another earlier denarius from Gnaius Lentulus circa 75 BCE in near mint condition with very little tarnishing and only a slight "horning" of iron oxide (a more leachable metal oxide that deteriorates at a faster rate of elemental mobilization) overlaying the silver in places. Since the Roman silver denarii were buried for at least two millennia in the Alps at about 1 meter depth in an equilibrium zone below surface groundwater and near bedrock but in silicate soil with good drainage, the minimal corrosion made them highly visible even in an ash lens and almost immediately datable.

Iron preservation in nearly any environment where even trace water is found in the liquid state is much more difficult because of iron's faster leaching rate in aqueous contexts. Iron oxide's molecular bond makes it particularly susceptible to elemental mobility via the agency of water. As Stanford students annually discover in the Alpine Archaeology course (where, among other topics, materials survival is studied as part of this course implementing archaeological science), controlled experiments with burying modern steel nails - even galvanized - for example, in Palo Alto hardpan clay for a few months during fairly dry California springs result in substantial iron oxide corrosion surface layers. Thus it is remarkable when our field teams in the Alps find ancient iron implements at a minimum 2200 meters elevation. In the case of our alpine field season in 2003, we excavated an almost nearly intact Roman iron double door latch hinge from circa 1st c CE at around a 70 cm depth.  This limited iron corrosion is again due to the combination of cold temperatures that inhibit diffusion and the fact that the majority of the water is in a frozen state for most of the past 2000 years.


*Organic Materials Survival*

Organic preservation is often also a resulting beneficial side effect of alpine altitude. As mentioned, the 1991 well-known discovery of Ice Man ("Ötzi") in the Otzal Alps of the Tyrol between Italy and Austria at around 3300 meters and around 5300 years BP [28] is another highly-published example of this state of preservation due to cold (Figure 6), where his wooden axe head and even the last meals of this Neolithic traveler were partly preserved as dietary artifacts in, among other things, fragmentary *Myxomycetes* bracket fungus used for a vermifuge and Neolithic wheat grain head with husks removed (known as *einkorn*) as a rudimentary cultivar. In the New World, as Johan Reinhard ahs found, Andean preservation of young Inca human sacrifices to the mountain gods from about 500 years ago at a far higher elevation (above 5000 m) although because it was frozen for only half a millennium, it shows similar frozen state low diffusion inhibiting decomposition in cryogenic-like circumstances. [29]

With increased glacial regression and recession as a function of global climatic change, more discoveries are likely to be found at higher Alpine altitudes. The Oztal group of Glaciers in the Austrian-Italian Tyrol where Ötzi was found in 1991 have seen a glacial retreat of 3.6-12.9 meters per year alone between 1910-1980 (and even greater recession rates since 1980).  Thus, what may be catastrophic for civilization could be good for archaeology. In other words, there will be more equally spectacular archaeological Alpine discoveries as glaciers continue to melt, although this is not a desirable payoff.

Nearly as important as Ötzi the Ice Man, in 2003 along the Schnidejoch ice field above Lenk (Bernese Oberland, Switzerland), another ± 4.700 year old deposit (circa 2700 BCE) Neolithic birch bark arrow-quiver was found in the receding ice field, along with other organic material intermittently exposed and then buried again under snow, including Bronze Age and Roman artifacts. [30] If actual global warming produces continued glacial thaw - although the opposite effect of another Little Ice Age similar to the early 19th century could also ensue if the Gulf Stream slows sufficiently - more spectacular organic finds in Alpine altitudes will be expected artifacts provided that decomposition does not occur first.

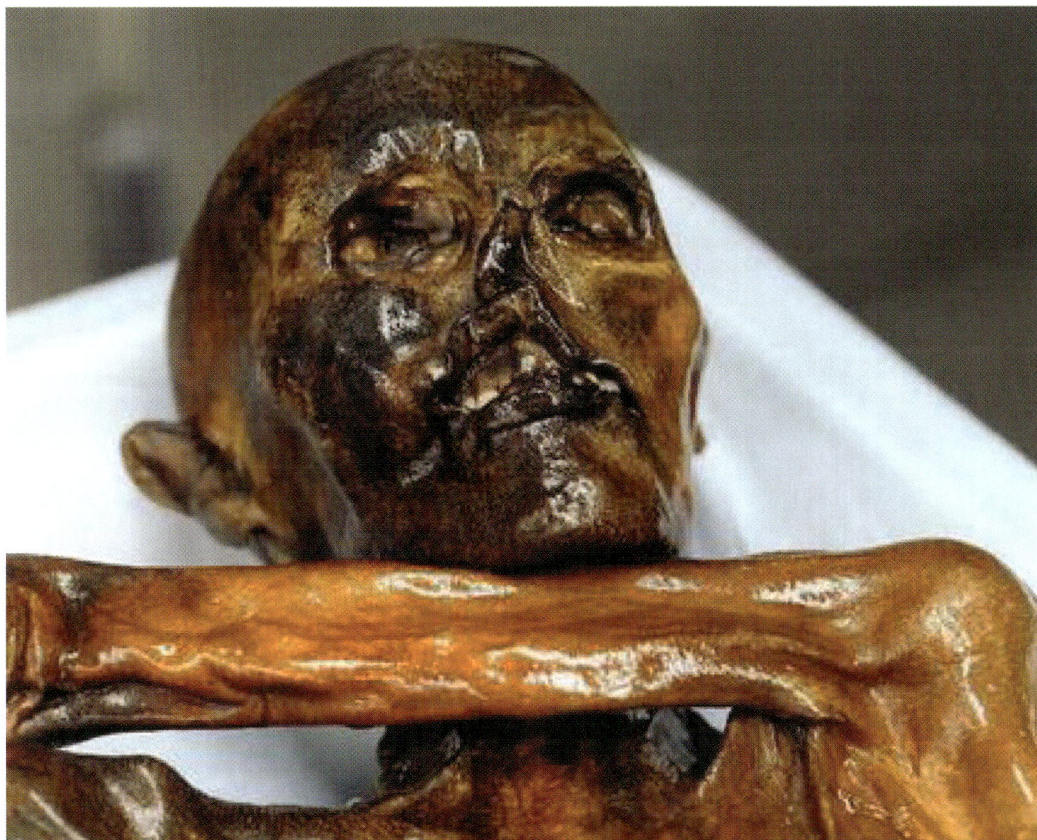

**6. ALPINE CLIMATE – OTZI ICEMAN 5300 YEARS BP/3300 BCE**

*Conclusion*

Overall, Alpine climate then often offers advantages for material preservation and disadvantages for locating and excavating material remains, (especially long-frozen organic material) becoming a proverbial two-edged sword for archaeological research. The Holocene (last 10,000 years) as a cultural repository of human prehistory and history may well be renamed the "Anthropocene" due to the human effects on climate change within that period since the last great ice age (often called the "Younger Dryas") when civilization from the rise of agriculture to metallurgy blossomed.[31] Although a rhetorical question with two possible answers, it becomes moot as to who can rightly determine which effect is better for archaeological practices: the disadvantages in excavation or the advantages for material preservation.

# Chapter Three

## ALPINE ARCHAEOLOGY: SOIL CHEMISTRY THEORY
## AND pH TESTING

### Introduction

Soil as artifact has not always been so obvious. Previous generations were often more focused on the objects embedded within soil rather than the soil itself as part of the archaeological record. This has changed greatly with application of pedology or soil science into archaeological inquiry.[32]  Partly because alpine soil can be so thin over bedrock, it is a vital part of field methodology to study alpine soil formation, deposition and characterization. Soil chemistry as derivable by pH analyses is part of that methodology in Alpine Archaeology.

For the last dozen or so years (1994-2007) our Stanford Alpine Archaeology Project has been conducting soil chemistry research as another method of characterizing archaeology microcontexts horizontally and microstratigraphy vertically.  As director of the project, my premise is that most of the existing methodologies for distinguishing microfeatures (part of overall micromorphology) in archaeology are visually dependent on physical characteristics. Some of these distinguishing factors include soil color (Munsell Charts), soil granularity (Wentworth-Udden grain size indices), and other somewhat quantifiable parameters such as soil texture as a function of particle symmetry or asymmetry along with homogeneity of grain size or lack thereof, soil compression as a function of density in cubic centimeters and soil moisture as measurable water content.  Pedology or soil science as a separate discipline is well researched with many directions in agriculture, forestry management and similar fields of study, and pH analyses is one of many such pedological evaluative instruments. This brief report explores this field application of pH field testing in experimental archaeology, especially in the Alps.

**7. pH ALPINE JUNIPER ON CARBONATE ROCK**

But utilizing soil chemistry as a further method to distinguish microcontexts and microstratigraphy in archaeology is, while uncommon, potentially beneficial for adding an invisible characterization to visible characterization. Taken all together, when reinforcing other characterizing methods, pH soil chemistry as one of many field tests has an immediate theoretical advantage in that it provides another method to complement, refine or even negate prior analyses in ways that merely visually-dependent field methods cannot.

As mentioned in Chapter One, flourishing plant habitats can often be good indicators of immediate local pH, (Figures 7 & 8) as both alpine juniper (alkali-loving) and alpine azalea (acid-loving) are found in abundance about 1000 ft below our excavations, whereas the immediate excavation site soil context is very close to a neutral 7.00 pH mostly derivable from the local schist geosol pH combined with organic matter.

Plants have long been recognized as clues to surface geology as well since calcium carbonate (e.g., limestone) will yield an alkali pH whereas granitic rock will often yield an acid pH. Both rock types are present in the alpine region of the Grand-St-Bernard pass but not in our immediate excavation vicinity. Alpine biodiversity represented in plant phytomass on the montane surface can then indicate the underlying geology and geomorphology, which can be very useful to archaeological research. [33]

## PREFERRED pH RANGES: SELECTED TREES & SHRUBS IN ALPINE CONTEXTS

| *Lower valley altitudes* | | | *Higher ridge altitudes* | | |
|---|---|---|---|---|---|
| Beech | (*Fagus*) | 6.0 - 7.0 | Azalea | (*Rhododendron*) | 4.5 - 6.0 |
| Birch | (*Betula*) | 5.0 - 6.0 | Fir | (*Abies*) | 5.0 - 6.0 |
| Elm | (*Ulmus*) | 6.0 - 8.0 | Juniper | (*Juniperus*) | 5.5 - 7.5 |
| Poplar | (*Populus*) | 6.0 - 8.0 | Pine | (*Pinus*) | 5.0 - 6.0 |
| Willow | (*Salix*) | 6.0 - 8.0 | Larch | (*Laryx-Larix*) | 4.5 - 6.0 |

8. pH ALPINE AZALEA ON ACIDIC/SILICATE ROCK

*Recent history of pH testing in Archaeology*

I first began suggesting and researching pH testing while at the Institute of Archaeology, London, in the 1980's and began experimentation with pH testing in 1993 in the Junipero Serra Park Project for the County of San Mateo. As field use was streamlined and incorporated into analyses, it was also found useful for short-term cultural resource management projects for the Stanford Management campus property consultancies between 1994-96 and subsequently elsewhere in the world including the Stanford Alpine Archaeology Project between 1994 to the present. Still theoretical, it has nonetheless yielded important new data in the field with portable pH testing equipment and is now a component of all my archaeological field research where applicable for soil chemistry.

Use of pH testing in archaeology is by no means isolated to my own field experiments. It has been used in Britain, Mexico, Indiana and elsewhere for some time and soil chemistry is but one of many analytical tools in archaeology: "Activities performed over long periods of time tend to leave soil chemical residues as evidence of those activities. Some of the questions studied in this chapter deal with the interpretive capabilities provided by chemical patterns." [34] Use of pH testing in archaeological field conditions has even been attempted for a possible explanation of why bones might survive better under certain soil conditions than in others. [35] In an exemplary text dealing with a broad spectrum of field analyses, Shackley posits that a high pH was destructive in diatom sampling of a Saxon-related context in Romney Marsh without providing the pH testing methods other than in indirect citation of field reports.[36] In an edited text on house activity areas, pH is one variable out of many used for "untangling complex formation" and "recognition of composite signatures". [37] Application in archaeology can be useful "when a genuine measured value is called for [where] it must be carried out using calibrated meter" as "one of the many stratigraphic characteristics that may be needed as part of the unraveling of site formation processes." [38] Elsewhere, Linda Manzanilla's projects at Teotihuacan, Mexico, have also used pH testing as one parameter of chemical testing of stucco floors (other analyses include testing for phosphates), where the activity of human-derived chemical alteration of such floor surfaces has been examined and quantified over years of testing. [39] Nonetheless, few excavation projects take soil chemistry seriously as they should, nor are pH analyses for macro or especially microstratigraphic differentiation used where it could be most useful, especially when other methods of micromorphology are less applicable due to visual stratigraphic homogeneity.

*Definitions of pH, geosols and archaeosols*

Some technical definition is necessary. What "pH" actually measures is "p" as a coefficient of the "H" (Hydrogen) on a scale from 0-14 where pH is the negative logarithm of hydrogen ion concentration (Figure 9). A reading of around 7 is neutral, 2-6 is acidic and above 7 (normally to 12 although the scale goes up to 14) is alkali (or basic). To be more precise, pH is expressed as the logarithm of the reciprocal of hydrogen-ion concentration in gram atoms per liter.[40] Each numeric value change, for example, from 5 to 6 pH means that a 5.0 ph is ten times more acid than a 6.0 ph; a reading of 9.0 pH is ten times more alkali than a pH of 8.0. Therefore, incremental change between soil pH readings of 6.8 to 7.2 in microcontexts is meaningful. This must be emphasized in archaeology where human-influenced change must usually be assumed.

## 9. The pH Scale

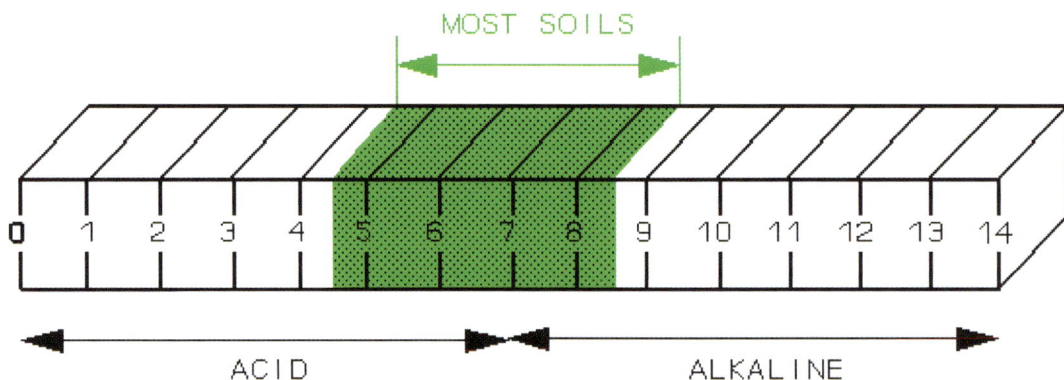

Values of pH below 2 and above 11 are generally inimical to life and are in fact toxic in high or low concentration at either end of the scale, therefore rarely found in nature. I have found most soils that support living organisms or are mostly derived from once-living organisms to be in the mid-range from 5-8. Soils as found in typical archaeological contexts (archaeosols) are most often mixtures of inorganic geological erosionally-derived elements (sand, gravel, etc.) and organic decomposition of dead matter, whether from plant and tree detritus, leaves, humus and other natural composting material of hydrocarbons (Carbon, Hydrogen, Oxygen and Nitrogen) and their oxides in the life cycle. Natural geosols are non-archaeological. Because our alpine contexts are at elevations (2200-2500 m) far above the tree line or timber biosomes (1900 m), our local soils (mostly shallow around a 1 meter depth over schist bedrock here), we do not encounter slightly acidic podzols as expected from the dominant larch conifer forest below where soil depth is greater (up to 2 m) above often similar neutral pH schist bedrock.

I have used a range of several portable pH field meters from fairly inexpensive (around $50.00 per meter) garden shop varieties (in California, Brookstone and Smith & Hawken Garden Supply) with only a simple 7.0 scale, as well as more reliable and more expensive (minimum $150.00 and up to $850.00 or more per meter) instruments from scientific supply houses (in California VWR Scientific) with a calibrated or adjustable 7.00 scale that can be made to account for temperature fluctuations. Specifications (product specs) of several portable pH meters used in my field research are found as an appendix to this brief report. Corning or IQ instruments make some of the most durable pH meters. For calibrating field results, which can be affected by temperature (very critical in the Alps), and maintaining sample purity as well as keeping the pH meter uncontaminated, it is necessary to regularly use a pre-determined manufactured buffer solution that will automatically pinpoint the pH meter's range and determine whether it has been skewed in any possible direction by the materials tested. Moderately sophisticated pH meters usually also give temperature readings in both Fahrenheit and Celsius readings. Because temperature, as mentioned, can skew results, we always either use pH-temperature conversion tables to factor this bias or use pH meters that have built-in features for temperature compensation and automatic conversion.

Over at least a decade, I have gradually constructed a field method whereby I can isolate the variables being tested – in this case different microsoils - by repeating my testing in the same way for the same time increments many times. Although yet an imperfect field methodology, for statistical accuracy I conduct multiple testing (minimum of three, preferably five different readings) per sample for representative sampling purposes. Results that are outside the cluster range of five testings are usually spurious.

As an example of pH soil testing I have reproduced a table of findings for one excavation context from data measured in 2000 in a collaborative project undertaken with the Soprintendenza of Val d'Aosta in the Plan of Jupiter. The findings are interpreted below this table.

### GSB-00  ROMAN STRUCTURE (MANSIO II? Unknown use)
### GRAN SAN BERNARDO – PLAN DE JUPITER 2000

### SITE pH ANALYSES

| Context | Volume | Time | Calibration [Buffer] | Solvent [$H_2O$] (Soil) | Material |
|---|---|---|---|---|---|
| S - 1 natural topsoil | 20ml | 2 min | 6.98 | 8.21 | 6.11 |
| O-O pulverized schist | 20ml | 2 min | 7.00 | 8.23 | 7.09 |
| W - 4 black soil | 20ml | 2 min | 7.00 | 8.07 | 6.74 |

| | | | | | |
|---|---|---|---|---|---|
| W - 17 yellow soil | 20ml | 2 min | 7.01 | 8.11 | 7.42 |
| N - 8 north wall | 20ml | 2 min | 7.05 | 8.02 | 7.57 |
| S - 5 south wall | 20ml | 2 min | 7.08 | 8.17 | 6.13 |
| E- 11 east wall | 20ml | 2 min | 7.05 | 8.21 | 8.31 |
| E - 11c east wall cement | 20ml | 2 min | 7.07 | 8.20 | 8.70 |
| D - 4 ash lens black | 20ml | 2 min | 7.09 | 8.17 | 8.61 |

As this above table shows, the methodology for each testing sample was repeated verbatim throughout to represent a testing constant. The control pH was a dual calibration method by testing first against the neutral buffer and second against the same water source (although a clean sample was taken from an ionized water source). The water served as a solvent to cleanse the pH probe electrode and was also utilized to create a soil suspension mix if our pH meter electrode so required a liquid measurement; dry and without the water calibration if the meter instead used a completely dry probe, but still cleansed with the water each time a sample was changed for new testing. Where possible, we used a pH meter that self-calibrated itself against temperature fluctuations, especially the more complex IQ-120 pH meter. The time tested (2 minutes) and volumetric variables (20 ml suspension or 20 ml dry volume depending on type of pH meter probe used) were also constant to better isolates the sample itself as the testable variable. We have found that the water used for cleansing the dry pH probe electrode does not at all affect the sample soil pH reading when the electrode is dried with one-use only acid-free neutral paper between each testing. We have also found that the water used for creating a suspension (10 ml soil, 10 ml water well mixed) does not bias the pH sample reading more than a potential variance of ±0.2 pH, which is insignificant because the accuracy of the pH meter is generally only at ±0.1 pH increments and the sample range pH variance between soils tested is generally far greater than ±0.2 pH per microstratigraphic sample context.

*Methodology and assumptions for interpreting sample pH*

The testable excavation context consisted of a walled room section of schist stones constructed in the Roman period intermixed with soil, 1st century CE judging by the artifacts. With the exception of two soil controls (non-archaeological topsoil and non-archaeological crushed schist, the primary geological agent of the local soil source) and one archaeological context from another trench (D-4 in Plan de Barasson) with a known ash lens, all other test loci represented on this table with the exception of S-1 were archaeological soil samples which had been freshly excavated as distributed around the trench at roughly the same depth of approximately 55 cm.

The range of buffer pH as control 1 exhibited a normal variance between 6.98-7.08 pH over a two-hour testing period with acceptably neutral results (variance of ± 0.10 pH. The pH range of ionized but local slightly alkali montane water from the purified spring closed source used as control 2 exhibited a normal variance between 8.02 and 8.21 with acceptably alkali results (variance of ±0.19 pH); as seen, the actual soil or context sampled showed a much greater variation (6.11-8.70 pH range, variance of 2.60 pH) as would be expected which greatly exceeded all other variables by at least a factor of 10 greater than the variance with the controls. Note all samples were tested at least five times for sample averaging. It is always necessary to remember that these variances between pH numbers represent a factor of 10 per each whole number change (e.g. 5.0 to 6.0 pH) for concentration of acid or alkali and therefore that what appears incremental can be nonetheless meaningful.

## Interpreting the sample pH as chemical characterization

*S-1 natural topsoil* (2-10 cm depth)          6.11 pH

This sample showed an acidic range pH most likely because of butyric acid exuded around the exposed root tips as a root growth product, an expected result with considerable vegetal material in this top natural stratum.

*O-O crushed schist*                          7.09 pH

This sample showed a fairly neutral range pH, also consistently sampled elsewhere for a stone comprised of a range of minerals from quartz and chlorite to mica. While this is the primary soil component, this is also serendipitous as a ternary soil control in that because it was natural, it also served to highlight the range of acidic and alkali sample readings as mostly derived from archaeological factors yet unknown but logically differentiated.

*W-4 black soil (west wall)*                   6.74 pH

This sample showed a slightly acidic range pH, but possibly darker than other microcontexts sampled and lower in pH value probably due to presence of less butyric acid than in S-1 but still measurable. This sample is definitely not from an ash lens with this low pH.

*W-17  yellow soil  (west wall)*                    7.42 pH

This sample showed a slightly alkali range pH which also complemented its yellow ochre color (modified Munsell Y3R2) characterization as different for unknown reasons; in other words both color and pH were in parity.

*N-8  north wall soil pH*                    7.57 pH

This sample showed a slightly alkali range pH which was indeterminate; we could not postulate any correlation here between pH, locus and color (modified Munsell Gray1Y2R2). There may also be marginal alkali elements mixed in residually as derived from the same sources (on a smaller scale) as samples E-11 and E-11c below.

*S-5  south wall soil pH*                    6.13 pH

This sample showed a fairly acidic pH range, and while not dark from butyric acid and too low for vegetal root acidity, was nonetheless not understood for its pH value other than to possibly illustrate the hypothesis that pH could differentiate microstratigraphy otherwise indeterminate from others.

*E-11  east wall soil*                    8.31 pH

This sample showed an alkali pH range and was very much taken from an area adjacent to the wall components. This is possibly high or alkali due to leaching concrete mixed into the adjacent soil.

*E-11c  Roman white cement in east wall*        8.70 pH

This sample showed a high alkali pH range and was taken directly from between stones as a whitish and chalky substance. That it is Roman concrete is first hypothetical and then a conclusion, not a presupposition, but its high pH appears to evidence this line of reasoning.  It was most likely imported limestone ($CaCO_3$) from a much lower altitude for just this purpose as a stone consolidant to hold schist wall stones together.

*D-4  ash lens*                                    8.61 pH

This sample was taken for comparison with an almost identical schist-derived soil with a known ash lens. The sample shows an alkali pH range as expected from carbonized organic material, most likely burnt roof timbers when the structure was destroyed in antiquity at an as-yet unknown date. Thus, while the ash lens was also dark in color like the topsoil, its color derives from completely different processes, demonstrating a chemical means to resolve color homogeneity.

### *Portable pH meter Product Specifications*

*I.  Mini Lab IQ120  (IQ Scientific Instruments)     VWR Scientific Supply*

Pocket-sized, waterproof pH meters with virtually unbreakable silicon chip ISFET pH sensors that store dry and need no maintenance. Both models feature a LCD display, automatic temperature compensation of 5°C to 40°C (40 to 105°F), a replaceable reference electrode, and long lithium battery life. Meters measure samples as small as a single drop.  Model IQ120 meter features one-point calibration for routine pH testing. Model IQ125 meter features automatic buffer recognition of three buffers (4.00, 7.00, and 10.00) and 1-, 2-, or 3-point calibration for high accuracy over a wide range of pH values. Range: 2.00 to 12.00 pH;  Resolution: 0.1 pH;  Accuracy: ±0.1 pH.   (Cost $179.00 in 2006).

*II. Corning Check-Mite pH Tester  pH-10 to pH-25  (Corning Instruments)   VWR Scientific Supply*

Portable microprocessor based pH meter in a waterproof and chemical resistant case; LCD readout 7.00 neutral calibration with buffer; Replaceable epoxy body, gel filled pH sensor; Auto calibration buffer recognition; pH 4, 7, 10.01 standards; Auto or manual 1 or 2 point calibration; Auto or Manual sample end-point determination; Standard replaceable lithium batteries. (Cost $45.00-85.00 in 2006).


***Conclusions:***

First, dark soil here is not necessarily an ash lens, but may also be a factor of organic butyric acid as pH testing shows. Same color but very different sources are given which visual characterization alone would not suffice to explain.

Second, Roman concrete, on the other hand, had a perfectly representative alkali pH as expected from primary $CaCO_3$ constituents of imported crushed lime, very anomalous in this montane environment of dominant neutral pH schist. It was actually a very good result where Roman concrete had only been suggested as a mortar here to consolidate schist stones but never actually proven until pH evidence was provided. Along with Roman tegulae roof tiles, the concrete mortar helps to interpret the structural Roman-ness of the context along with the Roman artifacts. Because the Romans only conquered the Salassi Celt tribe in the region in 25 BCE, the building is easily more datable to Roman or Gallo-Roman than to Celtic culture.

The hypothesis of the Alpine Archaeology Project was that application of pH testing validity in an archaeological context can be potentially used to differentiate microstratigraphy where pH is complementary with color and other characterizations or where it is difficult to differentiate microstratigraphy by color (where it is the same) and other characterizations. Our sampling and pH testing over several years suggests this hypothesis is valid.

Thus, on the one hand, validity of pH testing in archaeology may be optimal when used in micromorphology. Chemical testing by pH is especially useful to complement heterogeneous microstratigraphic and microcontextual elements. On the other hand, validity of pH testing in archaeology may also be optimal when used to differentiate homogenous microstratigraphic and microcontextual elements whose characterization may be better served by invisible soil chemistry than by mere visual characterization. Because application of soil chemistry pH in archaeology and specifically to micromorphology is still theoretical, it is expected that corrections of field methods and calibrations for pH testing will be forthcoming as assumptions are modified and pH testing processes are further refined.

# Chapter Four

# ALPINE GEOLOGY: PROVENANCING STONE
# FOR A JUPITER TEMPLE

## Introduction

Alpine geology is a complicated subject, usually defying generalizations.[41] Most geophysicists and geomorphologists believe that Alpine orogeny (mountain building) is a result of the collision between European and African tectonic plates in the Tertiary period that began around 65 million years ago and ended about 2 million years ago. Thus, the Alps are a relatively new mountain unit and much of what is visible in familiar Alpine topography, such as U-shaped montane valleys (as in Figure 10) is the result of erosion after being carved by great glaciers (in some places 1000 meters thick (3200 ft) and this late resulting state is less than 12,000-18,000 years old.

Early in the Tertiary period the enormous pressures of the slow continental collision resulted in gigantic broken folded layers with both near-vertical or horizontal upward-facing convex anticlinal folds and downward-facing concave synclinal folds. Some of these huge folds that stretch for miles are called *nappes* that have been forced through time to slide over great thrust faults. [42]

The Alps in the region under discussion here (Grand-St-Bernard Pass) are made up of mostly low-grade metamorphic rocks – like much of the Alps - such as schists and phyllites, although the local quartzite is a high-grade metamorphic rock. As a result of the slowly continuous continental collision, the Alps are still rising on an average of a few millimeters per year, although erosional forces and gravity continue to equalize this rise.

**10. ALPINE GEOMORPHOLOGY – ACUTE VARIATION AND ALTITUDE**

Finding the geological sources of archaeological materials is part of the larger picture of archaeological provenance. Closely related, archaeological prospection is a more general study [43] whereas finding stone sources via petrography (mineralogical determination by thin-sectioning) is the more specific type of analysis covered in this chapter. Although more about utilization of stone resources since prehistory, Archaeomineralogy is a relatively new and fascinating field in itself, [44] but is not the focus of this chapter. Specific examples of Alpine stone research where provenance questions have resulted in geological matches with the archaeological material include many different materials and time periods, for example, Neolithic greenstone axes from Western Alpine regions spread out between Northwest Italy (Piemonte) and Southeast France (Savoie) – some axes deriving from Alpine eclogites - [45] Alpine colored stone sources in the decorative Greek and Roman markets [46] as well as Austrian Alpine sources for locally-derived Roman marble artifacts at Faschendorf in Carinthia, a Roman burial area, [47] to name only a few such petrographic studies.

The Temple of Jupiter at the top of the Grand-St-Bernard Pass is mostly incomplete. The site was called Summus Poeninus (roughly translated as "Highest Poenine place") in the Roman Era, now located on the border between Italy and

11. ALPINE JUPITER TEMPLE

Switzerland but on the Italian side. Its stones have been robbed out for at least a millennium and it was presumably desecrated around 379 CE when the Christian Roman emperor Theodosius tried to wipe out paganism and relict Roman religion, if Augustine is credible (*De Civitate Dei* 5). We have attempted to reconstruct it theoretically (Figure 11) based on its 11 by 7 meter remnant shape carved in bedrock. Because the original stones of the temple are thus out of context, its scattered stones must be geologically identified and matched up first archaeologically, then it is possible to begin the search for a geological source in a quarry.

*Stone Provenance Criteria and Assumptions*

Field provenance of stone sources - matching archaeological and geological materials - can be successfully researched, especially when aided by a portable field petrography lab, excellent geological maps and a trained reconnaissance team using reliable field tests even in challenging topography and high altitude terrain. These requisites have been refined over several decades by this author in global montane contexts of stone provenance research, including the European Alps, Pentelic and other mountains in Greece and the Aegean Islands, Apennine Mountains of Italy, the Near East, Andes Mountains of Peru, and Tuxtlas and Sierra Madre Mountains of Mexico, among others.

The application of this field research has been conducted since 1994 in the Alps at the Grand-St-Bernard Pass. The Temple of Jupiter (11 x 7 meters) at Summus Poeninus was constructed around 70 CE at the summit of the Grand-St-Bernard pass between Switzerland and Italy at 2464 meters just over the Italian border in what was then a provincial outpost along the old Roman road *Via [per Alpis] Poenina* connecting the rest of the empire with Italy. The present remains consist now mostly of rock cuttings in the local schist with a few broken orthostats and many (at least 300) fragmentary ashlars of a whitish stone, identified in 1996 as calc-schist. The geological context of the Plan de Jupiter is a schist region where the Roman temple emplacement was close to a previous Celtic (Salassi tribe) sacred site with its high rock outcrop, now dominated by a late 19th c. bronze statue of St. Bernard.

The site of Summus Poeninus and its Alpine pass have been known and recorded at least since the mid-second century BCE by the historian Polybius; later recorded by Julius Caesar, the geographer Strabo and other Romans between the 1st c BCE to 2nd c. CE. This is the most important Alpine pass for direct north south connecting Italy with Gaul, Germany, Britain, although its elevation has usually been daunting along with its challenging weather year-round. [48]

*Geology of the Region and Field Methodology*

The summit of the Grand St Bernard Pass consists of an east-west saddle at the extreme western edge of the Pennine Alps. The Italian side then runs mostly southward and the Swiss side runs mostly northward. On the Italian side is a deep drop (roughly 400 meters) to a valley across which are the jagged peaks of Pain du Sucre at 2919 meters (quartzite), south of which is a gray calcium carbonate geomorphological ridge culminating in the Col du St Rhemy. In the Grand-St-Bernard pass saddle, at its west end across from the Pain du Sucre quartzite geomorph is the ridge of Petite Chenalette and the local micaschist geomorph of the Plan de Jupiter. [49] Between the western ridge of Petite Chenalette on the right and the quartzite ridge behind it - right at the horizon -

is a small pass (Fenetre de Ferret) at 2698 meters connecting Italy and Switzerland. In this small pass is a calc-schist quarry, sometimes used in more recent times as a sheepfold. This brief article describes the methodology and field results of the Stanford Alpine Archaeology Project between 1994-96 in searching for and locating that geological source of the stones of the Jupiter temple and related provenance of its stone. As often happens in mid-August (for example in 1995-1996, 1998, 2000-2003 a typical snowstorm left almost a foot of snow in the pass and still covered much of the Grand St. Bernard pass above 2500 meters a week later. It is not always easy to climb to the temple quarry in late summer and there is usually snow year round each year in shady parts near the summit of the Fenêtre de Ferret (2698 meters).

Given the intense metamorphosized folding of the Alps, a generalized geology of the Southwest Valais in the immediate region where we have conducted research since 1994 (locally only important for this study between Val Ferret, Mont Velan and Grand Combin) consists of Orsières granites and related gneisses in the northern Val d'Entremont; mostly phyllites and greenschist series between Mont Velan and Combes des Morts, especially in the local Chenalette and Mont Mort ridges on either side of the monastery and the pass saddle and quartzites and other depositions across the Italian border to the south of the pass summit in the Pain du Sucre ridges. Although there is considerable glacial moraine in the Val d'Entremont, glaciation in the immediate Grand-St-Bernard pass region has been intermittent – north to south or valley-oriented glacial striations are highly visible on nearly all the rocks in the Grand-St-Bernard - but no glaciers are known in the pass in the historic record since the Holocene (past 10,000 years). The Grand-St-Bernard Pass has been one of the primary Alpine routes since prehistory, even though year-round snow has often been present at the summit of 2472 meters (8200 ft.) and the higher nearby Fenêtre de Ferret at 2700 meters (9000 ft). Glaciers in the Alps have been carefully measured for over a century since the last Little Ice Age began to thaw around 1850. [50]

In 1994 our Stanford team first surveyed and examined the mostly whitish and yellow-tinged fragments of temple stone (length and width usually around 30-35 cm with 17-20 cm depth if intact) in the region. After determining it to be calc-schist [51] with a portable field lab for petrography pioneered by this researcher,[52] we searched for as much of the local worked remnants as possible, finding it emplaced as many as 200+ reused Roman ashlars in the mezzanine levels floors (Figure 12) and what is now below ground in subterranean vaults of the monastery Hospice du Grand-St-Bernard's Cave A & B (as in the fromagerie, Figure 13), the original vaulted rooms built by Bernard and his Augustinian monks in the late 11th century and in the succeeding several generations. Inside the monastery in the basement vault of cave A, the current fromagerie (cheese storage room with raised modern brick floor), our team found the original exterior 11th c. monastery doorway framed by Roman calc-schist temple stone with mica-schist built around it. The ground level of the monastery has risen at least 50 cm in the past millennium.

**12. JUPITER TEMPLE STONE IN MONASTERY FLOOR**

We also found temple stone fragments in various contexts on the temple plateau of the Plan de Jupiter, including these worked ashlars found together that can be seen in scale against a 40 cm measuring rod in fieldwork in 2000.

Our methodology for geological field-testing was fairly simple. Inside the monastery and its subterranean vaults, dark ash and carbonized material covered the medieval contexts. Again, reused stones ranged from across the Italian-Swiss border in ground contexts to re-emplacement in the medieval monastic structures, over a space of about 15 miles. We needed to determine which were local schist surfaces and which were reused Roman stones from the Jupiter temple.

Our field methodology included the following steps. We scraped off areas of ash and performed HCl (Hydrochloric) acid tests on part of every exposed stone surface. The silicate schist would not effervesce; the carbonate in the coarse-grained calc-schist would effervesce with its high calcium carbonate content (which also gave the whitish color).

We also conducted field scratch tests to differentiate softer carbonate calc-schist from harder quartzite silicates. This Roman white calc-schist is not to be confused with other much darker green chlorite calc-schists in the region with zoisite and epidote mineralography, some of which can be found 1 km north of the monastery. The local white quartzite - also a silicate, therefore it would not effervesce - was very similar in color with a yellowish tinge but its scratch hardness (about 7.0 on a relativized Mohs scale) precluded its use by the Romans around 70 CE.

We concluded that white or whitish stone would be preferable for the Romans and that the local greenschist was too friable and dark to be useful for much construction as would be suitable for a temple. Some of the known stone fragments were found as far away as Bourg-St-Pierre; others newly discovered littered the ground around the monastery and the Plan de Jupiter.

**13. JUPITER TEMPLE STONE IN MONASTERY VAULT**

The geomorphology of the Val d'Entremont region - of which the Grand St Bernard area is a part - divides between two large tectons, the Pennine Alps (with the local part of which consists mostly of phyllites and schists) and the Mont Blanc Massif (with the local part of which consists mostly of old granites and gneisses). The regional dividing line has created the Grand-St-Bernard pass route through the Val d'Entremont in its lower elevations. The town of Orsières lies at the junction of the Val d'Entremont (schists and phyllites) and the Val Ferret whose western edge is part of the Mont Blanc Massif (mostly granites at this point south of Champex-Lac).

In 1995 we began a topographic survey searching for the stone source, covering over 20 square miles of the local area involving hiking and climbing with geological testing equipment including the portable field petrography lab and HCl (hydrochloric acid) for spot testing. We covered the region and sampled as many as 120 small local microcontexts, including the basal talus slopes quartzite Pain du Sucre ridge, the Petite Chenalette, the gray carbonate San Rhemy ridge below the Gran San Bernardo valley, ranging from initial altitudes of 2200 meters to 2550 meters in elevation. At the same time, it seemed reasonable to assume that the Romans would not only look for a white, easily workable stone (unlike the hard white quartzite mostly unworkable to the Romans) but also be more likely to use a fairly local quarry higher than the temple placement for several reasons: I) if Jupiter were thought to "reside" in these stormy peaks, it would be higher, not lower; II) pragmatism suggested it would be easier to move stone down with gravity than up against gravity; III) given the challenging altitude and climate, the builders - who probably conscripted locals along with enslaved Salassi - would want to maximize local sources if available. The onset of early winter concluded our geological search in late August 1995 as we reached 2550 meters in the snowy valley below the Col du Ferret and Col du Fenêtre de Ferret where a fault zone separated surface quartzite and schist depositions.

## Fenêtre de Ferret Quarry

In 1996, a warmer summer in the Grand-St-Bernard region of the Pennine Alps, we resumed exploration of the valley below the Ferret passes and found what appeared to be the potential quarry was more recently reused as a sheepfold and shepherd's montane refuge of white softer stone in a geological zone of mixed schist and harder white quartzite just below the 2698 meter summit of the Fenêtre de Ferret along with the most likely route of moving the stones along greatly eroded residual transverse slopes. The natural 17-20 cm bedding planes of the quarry matched the measured depth of the intact temple ashlars. Because we had already tested the intact temple stones with HCl and these potential quarry stones also tested positive for carbonate with HCl, we

**14. ALPINE FIELD GEOLOGY**

took samples and made petrographic thin sections as well. As mentioned, in addition to HCl field testing for differentiating carbonate from silicate, field scratch tests were also used; carbonates could scratch easily with a steel knife blade; silicates like quartzite could not be scratched. Petrographic thin sectioning in the field followed these two simple field tests (as seen in Figure 14).

The petrographic match was close enough to be fairly certain. This hypothesis has subsequently proven reliable not only because no other known deposit of calc-schist occurs in the geomorphology of the region but also as semi-quantitative testing (including SEM with EDS, XRF and EPMA with yet unfinished tests) at Stanford University, USGS Menlo Park and the Institute of Archaeology, UCL, London, has gradually confirmed the petrographic match between the relict stone of the Jupiter temple and the quarry of the Col du Fenêtre de Ferret. Petrographic thins sections of calc schist and quartzite (Figure 15) highlight the mineral differences between these two local stones in cross-polarized light where they look superficially similar to the naked eye, despite their differences in hardness: calc-schist is about 3-5 on a relativized Mohs scale whereas quartzite is about 7.2 in relativized Mohs scale hardness.

The quarry at 2695 meter elevation measures around 3 x 5 meters in its reused refuge context, deeper than wide with scattered worked calc-schist blocks, often rough-dressed in the exact shape of the temple stones. The size of the blocks is critical: it is most likely the stone blocs were individually carried down the mountain from quarry to temple, as it would be difficult to transport more than one block at a time on the back of a porter due to the treacherous terrain with excessive abundant talus and altitude.

**15. PROVENANCE: CALC-SCHIST; QUARTZITE**

Additionally, because the small snow melt lake at the Plan de Jupiter had shrunk to the smallest levels in a ten year period in 2004, we were able to confirm over a hundred more previously unrecorded temple stone fragments in the lake margins and shallow water; again tested by HCl and field petrography to verify original temple context. As mentioned, the experimental field methodology and portable field lab used in this research has been extensively tested elsewhere by this researcher in global montane contexts. [53]

*Conclusions*

Field petrography, especially when examined with a portable optical petrology lab, can yield workable results for testing and even establishing the provenance of stone material by matching geological source to archaeological artifact. This is most suitable when not working with a single artifact (which would usually be difficult to establish with any degree of certainty) but, in the case of a whole structure - with many architectural members sufficient for representative statistical sampling – more easily matched to a quarry with a high volume of remaining geological source material as well. The difference between source provenance and find context can also yield important details about transport technology sometimes otherwise unavailable.

# Chapter Five

# ROMAN SPOLIA AT A MEDIEVAL CHURCH, BOURG-ST-PIERRE

## Introduction

Later reuse (spoliation) of Classical material is common wherever there is continuity between Roman and medieval communities, even when a considerable time has ensued between abandonment and reuse and/or when significant demographic change occurs. In the Grand St Bernard Pass region, the Parish Church of Bourg-St-Pierre and its vicinity in the alpine town of the same name (Figs 1-2) at around 1632 meters (5354 ft.) elevation in the Val d'Entremont of the Valais has many documented spolia on the route of the Grand-St-Bernard where the Roman route *of Via [in Alpis] Poenina* (as seen in the Peutinger Map) was succeeded by the medieval route of *Via Montis Jovis*.[54] The Stanford Alpine Archaeology Project has been studying and reconstructing Roman life in the upper montane Grand-St-Bernard pass, especially above 1600 meters elevation since 1995; reuse of Roman material in the region is especially significant in the monastery Hospice du Grand-St-Bernard from the 11th c. onward. [55]

## Definition and Philosophy of Spoliation

*Spolium* is defined here as a reused Roman artifact whose value for the medieval world lay in its obvious "Roman-ness" [56] - showing continuity between Classical Rome and Christian Rome - while at the same time demonstrating the break and conquest of the Christian world over Classical paganism. While there is precedent in Classical tradition for *spolia* over other cultures in a military triumph, the Judeo-Christian world and its biblical or other ancient antecedents find the same phenomenon in the literary record of the biblical I *Samuel* in the exemplum of conquest. When the victorious Philistines placed the captured Ark of the Covenant in the Dagon temple in Ashdod [I *Samuel* 5:1-5] or later when they placed the defeated Israelite King Saul's body on the walls of Beth Shean and his armor in the Temple of Astarte [I *Samuel* 31:10] they signified the triumph of their gods over the god of Israel, a temporary and dangerous display according to the biblical writers and theologians. At times spoliation may show a totemic desire to increase the sacredness of a new site by incorporating the sacredness of a prior site even if under different belief systems. Thus such a universal conquest tradition shows henotheistic propaganda value at the very least and religious dominance as a strong statement of religio-centrism alongside cultural hegemony by the conquering culture. Both somewhat polarized elements of continuity and conquest are evident in these spolia at Bourg-St-Pierre. These spolia are deliberately placed to be conspicuous from all sides of the church, as will be shown in the following discussion.

**16. TOWN OF BOURG-ST-PIERRE AT 1632 METERS**

For medieval Christianity, the philosophy of spoliation – while at times a merely pragmatic reuse of good Roman material for time and energy conservation - is not difficult to trace. When the ultimate motives are examined for reuse of Roman material as spolia beyond the specific parish church of Bourg-St-Pierre (its clocher or bell tower visible in Figure 16) and in a medieval world at large, perhaps it is Christian triumph over former Roman persecution that is seen in the biblical passage of *Epistle to the Colossians* 2: 15. "He disarmed the rulers and authorities and made a public example of such, leading them in triumph [*thriambeusas* in Greek] over them in it." Combining pragmatism with conquest, similar examples exist throughout the former Roman world, "appreciating and appropriating the past" as in Hexham abbey church, Britain: "building a monument to honor the new authority in Britain using the most opulent remains of the old authority. Such symbolism would not have been lost on the people of Britain...Roman masonry represented far more than its simple utility as building material. It symbolized the continuing legitimacy of the greatest power that Europe had ever known." [57] As mentioned, this is philosophically compounded when there is sacred continuity even in the purported conquest of paganism by Christianity (the "my god is bigger than your god" credo).

Some of these specific spolia in Bourg-St-Pierre to be discussed in the following sections are noted already in the prior literature but reappraisal shows more can be documented especially in the area immediate to the parish church, a most likely place of display given the above.

### *Relevant History of Bourg-St-Pierre*

The history of Bourg-St-Pierre is known from village and cantonal archives dating to the 8th c., although it is likely that a Roman *mansio* (roadside hostel) logically existed here in the 1st c. CE halfway between the Roman town of *Forum Claudii Vallensium* and the *Summus Poeninus* sanctuary and *mansiones*. Charlemagne also passed through here in 800 en route to Mediolanum (Milan), and a subsequent Carolingian castellum appears to have been built - possibly over a Celtic oppidum - on the hill above the town along with a Carolingian chapel and adjoining small monastery were established in the town under the Abbé Vultgarius whose death is recorded here between 812 and 820 CE as Monastère Saint-Pierre de Mont-Joux [58] whose clerical Petrine motif of crossed keys is retained in the town heraldry.

This Carolingian history evidences the early preeminence of Bourg-St-Pierre [59] over the later and ultimately more important 11th. c. Hospice du Grand-St-Bernard at the summit of the pass. Between the 9th and 11th c., most of the pass, including the much higher summit with its hostile climate, was reputedly in the hands of Saracens or brigands. [60]

Bernard of Menthon as Archdeacon of Aosta (subsequently canonized as St. Bernard) sought later to reduce such threats for travelers through the mountains in need of protection against such human elements as well as the fiercely inclement weather so common in the Pennine Alps on any given day of the year. [61]

### Constantinian Milestone

Between CE 308-311 an imperial milestone was set up in a column of local gneiss from the Val d'Entremont at the summit of the pass which records, among other things, the distance as 24 Roman miles as between the summit and *Forum Claudii Vallensium* [Martigny], as the epigraphic abbreviation reads *XXIIII F C VAL*. This 2.5 meter high milestone actually belongs at the summit but was apparently moved down the mountain to the site of Bourg-St-Pierre (St. Pierre de Mont Joux), apparently by Charlemagne's consent in the 9th c. with the installation of the monastery there. The evidence of this relocation to the NE church corner (Figure 17) lies in the fact that it is 24 Roman miles between the summit and Martigny along the old Roman road but only 16 Roman miles between Bourg-St-Pierre and Martigny where the milestone now stands in Bourg-St-Pierre. The milestone, as noted, is now incorporated into the northeast side of

**17. ALPINE SPOLIA MILESTONE**

the realigned churchyard of the transformed Carolingian chapel adjacent to the old apse, which was later altered to be the transept of the later church with its newer 11th c. church clocher or bell tower. The milestone is most noticeable along the ancient road that runs through the village, which route it faces from the churchyard. Roman milestones are often reused as spolia elsewhere in Europe, notable ones in the Valais include several other local milestones incorporated into the 9th. c. Abbey of St. Maurice in the clocher fenestra, one in the apse of the 10th. c. phase of the Cathedral of Martigny, and one in the courtyard of the 13th c. Savoyard Castle of Aigle in Vaud. The fact that these milestones were originally secular emblems of imperial power is important for their subsequent Christianization by assimilation into sacred Christian contexts.

## Column Fragments in Church Clocher Tower – Fenestra Decoration

Likewise in the 11th c. clocher or bell tower of the Bourg-St-Pierre parish church are four Romanesque fenestra whose arches are separated by fragmentary Roman columns in the Tuscan order, presumably from the Jupiter Poeninus temple ruins in the pass. Each of the four column fragments - ranging from a length of 0.6 m to 1.2 m - matches petrographically to the other Roman *"marmor"* [actually calc-schist from Fenêtre de Ferret] from the Jupiter Poeninus temple remains in the monastery hospice and the quarry source on the Fenêtre de Ferret pass above the monastery and the Grand-St-Bernard valley [62] as already noted. Their placement in Bourg-St-Pierre has always been assumed to be contemporaneous with the other Roman monuments described below, i.e., assimilated in the 9th c. into parish precincts. These calc-schist column fragments of a uniform stone can be measured around an average of 48 cm in diameter at the base, although with the obvious variations seen, they could all be from the same original column but different portions thereof. The column fragments can be easily seen from all four sides of the churchyard as the clocher towers above the medieval town. Again, other similar examples of fragmentary columns used in double-arched fenestra are seen at the Abbey Church of St-Maurice and elsewhere in the Valais. [63]


### Re-used Jardinière Column bases

On top of the parallel gates to the small communal *campo santo* cemetery within the sacred area or enclosure adjacent to the parish church are two jardinières whose roughly 55 cm diameter bases appear to be column capitals turned upside down. This small gate leads toward the parish priest's domicile to the immediate west of the cemetery. It is doubtful that these are geologically or materially connected to the crude jardinières themselves, that is, the jardinières are of a different geological carbonate material and color than the bases [which appear to be originally used as Tuscan order capitals and thus most easily understood as Roman], which accentuates their use as spolia.

The function as jardinière bases here is seen as a use for a pair of objects whose installation on top of square pedestals makes them the most visible emblems of Roman artifacts on the western side of the cemetery, thus making a symmetrical statement on each side of the churchyard with identifiable Roman spolia. That is, the fenestra column fragments in the clocher tower can be seen from all directions, including the north, whereas the milestone can be best seen along the ancient and modern road from the east side of the church and the epigraphic fragments and marble blocks can be best seen from the south side of the church. That the column bases of the jardinières are over a gateway makes them even more noticeable at the west churchyard portal.

While there are other gateways in the churchyard, at least two of the others also have spolia associated with them: the milestone with the churchyard east gate into the ancient road and the following epigraphic fragments and temple blocks with the churchyard south gate into the ancient road. This conspicuous placement of the spolia at the four churchyard corners is deliberate. The north-facing gate is the only one apparently bereft at present, but closer examination of this context may yield additional spolia.

### Church Courtyard Epigraphic and Other Ashlar Fragments

It is unknown whether or not these spolia (Figure 18) are in their original secondary placement contexts [with the first placement being the ancient Roman use], although since most of the original medieval structures are now either lost or modified beyond recognition, some may be in tertiary reuse. The notable epigraphic fragments [PO]NTIF [EX] (6.5 cm high) part of an imperial title for chief high priest of the secular Roman state religion as *Pontifex Maximus* - and *VESP[ASIANUS]* (14.5 cm high) [64] - the founding emperor-general of the Flavian dynasty c. CE 69 are most interesting for the prominence given them along the public right of way in the later Baroque context, which may well be a repeat of the medieval reuse or at least equally prominent to the view of townspeople then as now. [65]

**18. ROMAN EPIGRAPHY ORIGINALLY FROM SUMMIT**

At least 20 other Roman "*marmor*" blocks (although calc-schist and therefore not marble at all) plus fragments can also be counted here. They are cemented into a sloping pavement with three additional fragmentary stumps of columns, and the middle column fragment has a flange or ring, also cemented in the sloped wall of the church cemetery. It is also evident that the ground level has risen where the blocks are reused relative to the original ground plane at cemetery level in which they are now cemented, which suggests late medieval reuse when the church was modified (1739) in both size and axis of placement.

Although there is a considerable slope gradient from a higher eastern edge to a lower western edge in the town itself, the fact that the roadway has risen 1.3 m over time relative to the cemetery suggests that the old churchyard is closer to the ancient ground level here. It is not known when or where the spolia were used after the 9th c. The spolia employed around the churchyard, with the exception of the 11th c. church clocher tower and possibly even the milestone, are possibly in tertiary reuse locations and may even date in partial reuse to Baroque renovation when the old parish church was enlarged and its axis changed from north/south to east/west in 1739. The most likely chronology of initial spolia use would be a *terminus post quem* between the 9th c. and an 11-12th c. *terminus ante quem*, after which date the new hospice monastery of Bernard at the summit of the pass almost 1000 meters higher would have and did use other spolia in prominent display.

The parish church of Bourg-St-Pierre is an ideal location to display Roman spolia en route to and from Italy in the medieval world, both as a reminder of former imperial Roman control even in the mountains of Valais and as a Carolingian reminder of Christian conquest over Roman paganism. Although the ecclesiastic center of the town has remained in roughly the same place since the 9th c., however greatly altered (even possibly reusing a Roman *mansio* station along the Via Poenina), additional medieval remains in the town are visible to the south on and near the summit of the hill (1689 m) above the alpine garden La Linnea, both of which contexts were castle defense structures (including hexagonal tower remains with arrow loops approximately 10 meters high, and the highest of which - almost completely destroyed ("Le Chateau") - may even reuse a Celtic hill-fort (*oppidum*) site, giving the name of Bourg to this town already identified with St. Peter. Thus, continuity and conquest were emphasized to medieval residents here in this village and to travelers on the Alpine pilgrim route through this place with a known Carolingian history and what may be the earliest monastery in the Val d'Entremont.

*Conclusions*

In conclusion, these Roman spolia in Bourg-St-Pierre function more as a philosophic statement of conquest than in any practicality of convenient reuse, particularly when the medieval town of Bourg-St-Pierre is mostly constructed with easily-obtainable local schist and gneiss rather than the Roman material from the summit eight miles up the road and from an elevation of almost four thousand feet higher. [66] In a way consonant to medieval syncretistic thinking, the very storm god of the ancient mountain pass, Jupiter Poeninus himself, is tamed thereby. The deliberate placement of these spolia around the churchyard can be seen as a new Christian topos replacing the old pagan one with conspicuous emphasis, since it could also be said that practical use was spurned in not having any structural function but that of display only to show the ultimate triumph of Christian conquest over once-great but now humbled pagan Rome.

# Chapter Six

## ALPINE ROMAN ROADS IN GRAND-ST-BERNARD PASS

### Introduction

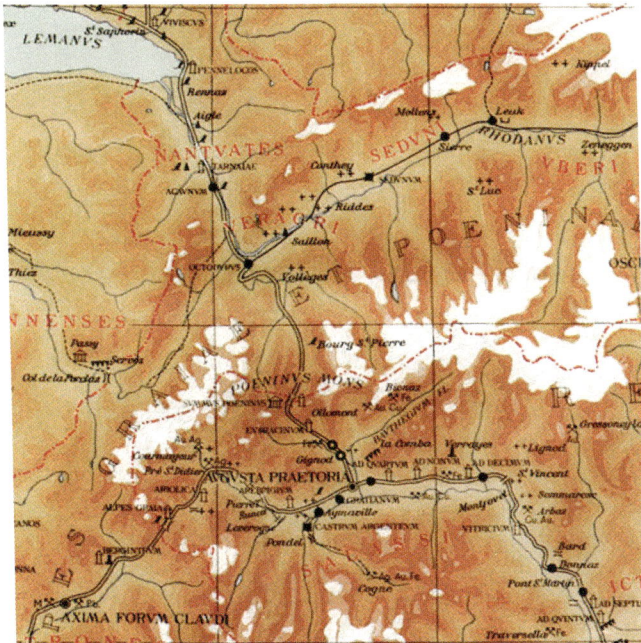

**19. ALPINE ROMAN ROADS MAP**

In 1994 the Stanford Alpine Archaeology Project began research to examine Alpine Roman Roads in the Grand-St-Bernard pass between Aosta, Italy and Martigny, Switzerland. This research has been conducted under the auspices of Stanford and the Office du Recherche Archeologique, Valais, Switzerland, and the Soprintendenza for Archaeology of the Aosta Valley, Italy. There is an international collaborative effort at present between Italian and Swiss archaeological authorities to bring together years of research in the Great St Bernard Pass. For over 30 years Francois Wiblé has undertaken the highest calibre archaeological research in Martigny and is the undisputed authority on Roman presence in Valais. Italian archaeologists have also conducted much archaeological research in the Plan de Jupiter and this ongoing work will present the most complete picture when soon published. The author expresses his appreciation to the Canton of Valais, Office du Recherche Archeologique, especially Francois Wiblé, Cantonal

Archaeologist, and the Valle da Aosta, Soprintendenza for Archaeology, specifically to principal archaeologists Lorenzo Apollonia and Patrizia Framarin, for their support in conducting research in this region.

Because many of the prior studies on Roman roads in the Alps and this pass in the Pennine Alps in particular have already been long published in Italian, French and German, the Stanford research noted here is much indebted to these foundational studies by authors noted below. The Stanford study of the Roman road in the Pennine Alps (*Via per Alpis Poenina*) is then only original in part, and while new findings are briefly summarized here, the Stanford project primarily seeks to make available the existing literature to an English-speaking audience. Some of the prior literature includes articles or monographs by Blondel (1962),[67] Walser (1984),[68] Wiblé (1975-2006),[69] Planta (1979),[70] Mollo Mazzena (1991)[71] and many others, including the seminal work in English by W.W. Hyde, *Roman Alpine Roads* (1935),[72] excellent but now outdated. The new and original research of the Stanford group is also summarized here, and published elsewhere in part, for example, in the *Journal of Roman Archaeology* XI (1998) by this author.[73] This brief summary is not offered as comprehensive about all Roman roads in the Alps, but mostly considers one region of the Pennine Alps.

## Roman Roads: Principles and Common Features

Several fundamental principles of Roman roads are applicable to Alpine roads: 1) roads can be made up of many surface materials including stone, gravel, packed earth, wood, sand and other components and are often layered, but not necessarily so in the Alps; 2) milestones often marked distances between Roman towns but were most likely sporadic rather than placed at regular intervals; 3) roads were often cambered (rounded) and sometimes with a central spine (*spinum*) and tapered edges to facilitate drainage to the sides; 4) large terrace wall stones (*ambonae*) can help anchor a road in place on a slope with a steep gradient or act to build up a road bed in rocky terrain; 5) as in many rural or remote locations, roads are rarely more than 3 meters in width; 6) public inns or private way stations and hostels (*mansiones*) were usually distributed at a distance of a typical day's journey every 25 miles in valleys or flat places; 6) roads are generally placed where there is little danger of flooding, in this case higher up in a valley rather than on the valley floor; 7) where the terrain crosses wet or unstable ground, a raised road bed (*agger*) is often constructed; 8) in urban contexts the road is more likely to be of harder stone; whereas in remote or rural contexts as in the Alps, the roadway can sometimes be not much more than a track or path.

### Roman Road Fallacies

The old assumptions - usually fallacies - about Roman roads are clearly not applicable or demonstrable in these mountains: such Roman roads are not straight and are not laid down in four strata, as some have misinterpreted Vitruvius in his *De Architectura* about *pavimentum* elsewhere. Nor are Roman road ruts (ground down through time by iron wheel rims) uniform in width in these Alps.

For example, there are clear road ruts in the Donnas rock-cut road in the Aosta valley: they are mostly 130 cm apart, suggesting the axle width here of a certain unspecified type of Roman cart; there is no exact standard scale Roman road rut as some believe applicable uniformly everywhere, as we have observed a rut width range from 120-140 cm. It is illogical to expect that all Roman vehicles always adhered to a uniform axle width, and even the possibility of legislating such would be unlikely to be enforceable across the Roman world, especially in remote areas like the Alps.

For overall general utility, the brief summary of Roman roads by Casson (1974)[74] remains useful. Chevallier's work (1976)[75] is comprehensive about Roman roads in general. Brief as it is, Hamey and Hamey's illustrated text (1981)[76] is also helpful.

## *Features of Roman Alpine Roads*

In addition, Alpine contexts offer differences or modifications to the montane landscape not found in Roman roads on flat plains. Some of the most interesting Alpine Roman road modifications include the following, especially in the Grand St Bernard Pass and Valle da Aosta:

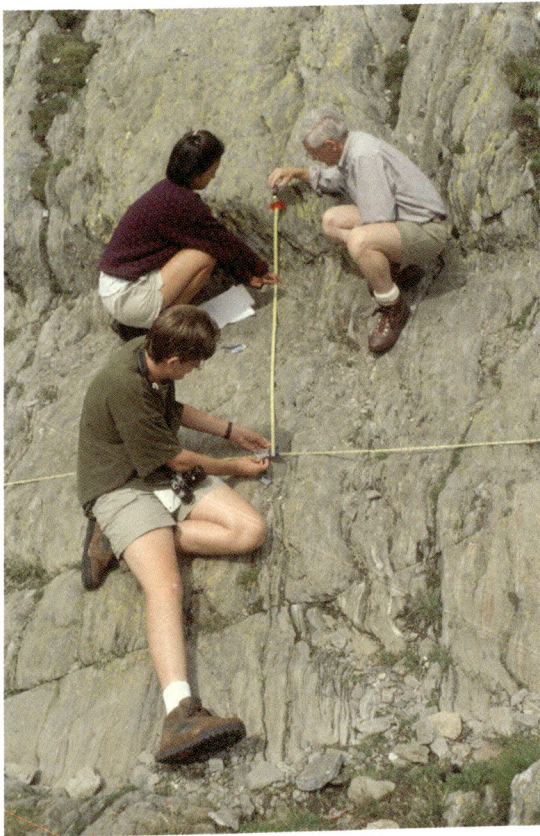

20. ALPINE ROAD STANFORD ARCHAEOLOGY TEAM 1994

1) Often daunting and spectacular rock-cut road beds carved in bedrock can be found in several contexts in these Alps, for example, including at the summit of Roman Summus Poeninus (Figure 20) at the top of the Grand-St-Bernard Pass (2472 meters, 8200 ft. elevation) and at Donnas along the Dora Balthea river downriver of Aosta in the Valle da Aosta.

2) Roman roads in these mountains were usually planned and constructed on the sunnier sides of valleys to avoid permanent or long-term snow in shadow of high ridges and were often higher up on valley sides to avoid the rush of snowmelt streams.

3) Wooden beams to support planks appear to have been inserted into sockets carved into bedrock, ostensibly for a wooden plank road section over plunging or irregular terrain.

70

4) The rock-cut road section at Summus Poeninus at 8200 ft also dovetails into a geological fault at an acute angle of around 105 ° (Figure 21), which fact has allowed the Stanford project to make a discovery: previously it was assumed that pivoting front axles on wagons were not introduced until around 100 AD/CE according to K. D. White (1989),[77] whereas this rock-cut roadbed appears to roughly antedate this date by as much as a quarter to half century.

**21. ALPINE ROCK CUT ROAD ANGLE**

5) This Roman road (*Via per Alpis Poenina*) covers in 3.5 broad curves what the modern road built around 1900 covers in 22.5 switchbacks, with the Roman road often having a gradient of 19.8 % in its steepest sections, making oxcarts with yokes very problematic, as Strabo mentions (4.6.7-12) even before the likely road cuts were finished somewhere between CE 42-70 or the Claudian and Vespasianic eras as the most likely dating of this road section.

6) There are also sections with steps carved into the bedrock in the Combe de Mort-Combe de Barasson confluence, possibly for pedestrian traffic while alternate sections were for pack animals and carriages.

7) One very important milestone, as already discussed in the previous chapter, is now at Bourg-St-Pierre, connected to the medieval church corner, and used as a *spolium* (trophy) because it is dated to Constantine circa 308-311 CE and lists the distance in Roman miles from Summus Poeninus to *Forum Claudii Vallensium* (Martigny) as 24 Roman miles: *F C Val XXIIII*. It clearly belongs at the summit because it is now only a distance of around 17 Roman miles from Martigny.

8) Because of the vertical climb, Alpine mansiones or road stations are not separated by day journey distances of 25 Roman miles but rather half the distance at around 12-13 Roman miles, as shown on the *Tabula Peutinger* at the site of *Eudracinum* (San Rhemy) from Summus Poeninus (*Eudracinum XIII in Summo Poenino*) on the present Italian side of the pass; probably also to be found near or at Bourg-St-Pierre on the Swiss side. While not a mansio as far as we know, the likely Roman refuge at Plan de Barasson may have also served as a way station in inclement weather, as it is situated just below the most arduous ascent on the Swiss side at the margin of where the worst weather would linger in the aptly-named Combe de Mort.

9) In the Combe de Mort (around 7800 ft or 2300 m), a road section with relict terrace wall stones (*ambonae*) also follows the sunnier eastern side of the narrow valley.

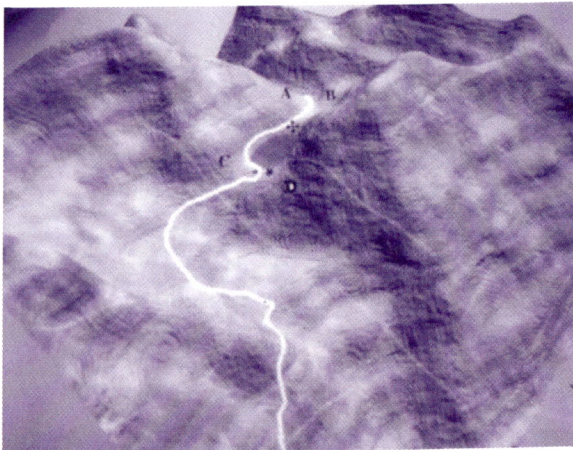

**22. ALPINE GSB ROAD DESCENT**

A small lake lies between the two countries of Italy and Switzerland on the present international border; the Swiss side is notable for the Monastery-Hospice du Grand-St-Bernard. The steepest gradient of 19.8% lies just below the Italian summit and scarp to about 2300 meters (Figure 22) and then a less steep gradient (10%) continues for much of the distance down to the bottom of the Gran San Bernardo valley to about 2100 meters elevation, after which it steeply drops again at a gradient of about 16-18% all the way down to 1400 meters elevation above the village of San Rhemy. As mentioned, the modern road - not seen here - covers in 22 switchbacks over 2000 vertical feet and a few linear kilometers the same distance the Roman road covered in three broad curves.

## Excavation of a Roman Road context in Combe de Mort

In 1997 with permission from the Office du Recherche Archeologique of the Canton of Valais, the Stanford Alpine Archaeology Project conducted a small excavation across the identified context of the Roman road (*Via per Alpis Poenina*) where the rocks closed the pathway on all sides in a spot (Figure 23) identified by Planta in 1979 as the most likely road route at an elevation of around 2400 m (8000 ft.). Stratum A was turf and roots (top 15 cm), Stratum B was small flat schist stones (15-30 cm depth) mixed with gravel, Stratum C was a mixture of clay and montane schist soil (25-58 cm depth), the clay most likely imported, Stratum D was bedrock and on the side (without fossa ditches) Stratum E was made of possible terrace

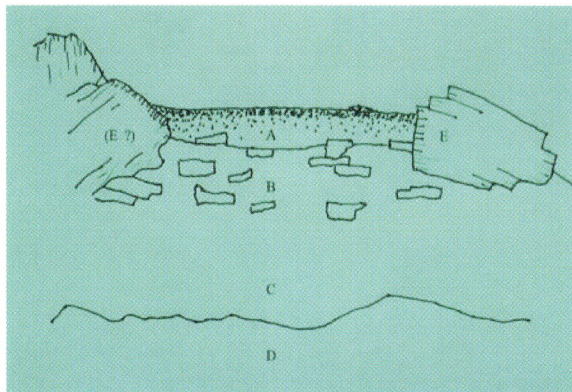

**23. ALPINE ROAD EXCAVATION X-SECTION**

stones (*ambonae*) containing the road on at least one side with potential rock fall (also noted as Stratum E) on the other side. Because the putative Roman road here is narrow than expected (at least 2.8 m width would be more typical), and the total passage through the rocks here is constricted at this point to around 2.7 m, what is tentatively identified as *ambonae* terracing on either side may in fact be a consequence of natural montane rock movement on one or the other *ambonae* terrace. There may or may not have been a *fossa* (drainage ditch) as well on the right side but a combination of intermittent erosion and alluviation made this difficult to confirm after several millennia. There were both medieval and Napoleonic (c. 1800) refurbishing of sections of the primary route of Via per Alpis Poenina, but most unlikely in this one excavated context since an alternate stone-paved route lies about 200 m to the south and built up along a cliff mostly in shadow, which the Roman engineers appear to have avoided for risks of avalanche and deep snow.

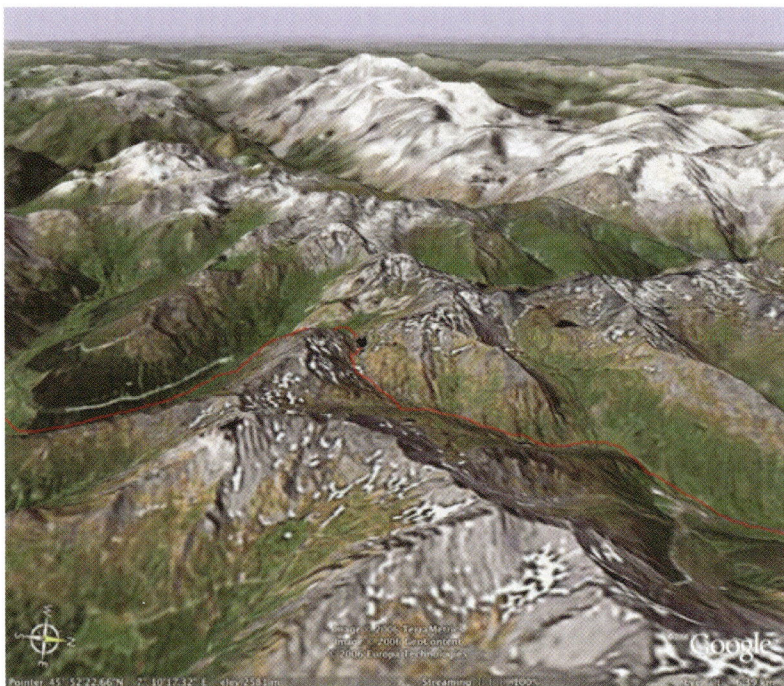

**24. ALPINE ROUTE GSB PASS**

The Roman road through the Grand-St-Bernard Pass most likely followed a route that can be reconstructed (or very close thereto) for much of the way en route between Forum Claudii Vallensium (Martigny) and Augusta Praetoria (Aosta). The distance covered between the two ancient Roman cities is only about 49 kms. As a reminder of how much work - possibly using conscripted or enslaved local Celtic (Salassi) labor - was involved in these Alpine rock-cut road sections, the schist bedrock had to be chiseled out by hand with metal tools, often to the depth of nearly a full meter in the case of the road sections visibly rock-cut on the Plan de Jupiter on the Italian side of the Grand-St-Bernard pass. While the context schist has a relative Mohs scale intermittent hardness around 3-5, this would still most likely require iron tools and was a formidable undertaking for its engineering achievement. Along this Roman road (Figure 24) that stretches over 49 kms from Aosta (Roman Augusta Praetoria) in present Italy to Martigny (Celtic Octodurus and Roman Forum Claudii Vallensium) in Switzerland, we have excavated since 1996 part of the relict crude Roman road bed (Figure 25) around 2380 meters elevation as well as the lower elevation small Roman or Gallo-Roman refuge (or small *mansio*) in the Plan de Barasson about 2270 meters elevation that was watered by a rock-carved aqueduct from a higher tarn lake about 2 kms away.

**25. ALPINE ROAD EXCAVATION – P. HUNT**

## Conclusions

In conclusion, in terms of Roman Alpine road building, it should be understood that whatever pathways Romans used – especially in the Alps - can be properly titled Roman roads, regardless of how they do or do not conform to Roman roads elsewhere. Roman roads cut through rock are not the norm anywhere, and while Alpine Roman roads do not substantially differ, there are more than a few Roman road sections in the Alps that do, in fact, cut directly through bedrock in difficult terrain where there is no other way around the ubiquitous stone at the surface.

# Chapter Seven

## ALPINE GALLO-ROMAN HYBRID MATERIAL CULTURE

### Introduction

Several questions have been foremost since the outset of our fieldwork and research in the Grand-St-Bernard Pass in 1994, especially inquiries about life between the 2nd century BCE and the 4th century CE, a region between the Mont Blanc Massif and the Pennine Alps. How deep was Romanization in this remote, high altitude (1600-2700 meters, 5300-9000 ft.)? Alpine region and can this idea of possibly superficial Romanization be extrapolated into other remote regions such as Roman frontier *limes*? What are some potential reasons for cultural hybridization between Roman and Celts and how much of this hybridity was in both directions? How might the archaeological evidence provide possible answers to these questions? These may appear to be simple questions, but they have perplexingly complex answers, only of few of which can be presented here, and considerable ramifications for further study. Some of the methodology (for example, examining material evidence) in attempting to answer questions posed here builds upon previous studies,[78] but this brief chapter will more likely pose tentative ideas rather than offer any solid conclusions.

Historic reasons suggested for cultural hybridity are often one-sided, perceived in one direction only, where hybridity is likely to be rarely unidirectional. Roman assimilation of surrounding cultures is understood to be a well-known phenomenon, although what we infer from ancient authors like Lucan may not always be so warranted on closer inspection [79] along with Caesar's sometimes-dubious accounts of Celtic religion. Roman absorption of Celtic deities or religion (e.g., *Mars Toutatis*, *Minerva Sulis* or, in our local region, *Jupiter Poeninus*) can not only serve both cultures but also avoids Roman offense of local peoples and is at the same time benignly superstitious on the part of the Romans as not wanting to offend possible deities. On the other hand, it is accepted that Celtic assimilation of Greco-Roman culture follows several traditional patterns and probable causes: desire for greater status amongst themselves as well as with Romans, practicality in economic matters including trade, imitation as the sincerest form of flattery, and resignation to conquest, among many other possibilities. Extent of "Roman-ness" itself in the Alps, let alone the Roman Empire, is a huge topic best considered elsewhere beyond the scope of this chapter.[80]

The Alps were a natural frontier for both Romans and Celtic tribes, a cultural nexus where near-constant contact from around the 2nd century BCE onward resulted in transition and hybridity, as surviving material culture shows. While deity names and apparatus have been long assumed to reflect this hybridity, additional material evidence for this Gallo-Roman cultural mixing can be easily demonstrated in Celtic coinage, for example, by Sequani and other tribes, where a brief numismatic tradition copies Greek and Roman types; also in architecture and in ceramic artifacts where local *terra sigillata* and Vindonissa ware, for example, adopt and adapt Roman models; as well as in the obvious stamped *tegulae* (Roman roof tiles) and less obvious *tabulae ansatae* votive material in bronze, silver and gold plaques.

## Hybrid Religion

The local Celtic mountain god in the Grand-St-Bernard region was presumably a god of the Salassi tribe whose territory it was before Roman conquest, but was also likely to be a deity across the Alps and elsewhere in Celtic domains. This mountain and storm god was named *Pen* or *Penn*, most likely meaning something to do with a "high place" in the local Salassi Celtic dialect. There was, according to Hyde, a likely *columna solis* or sun column shrine to this god along with the sun god badly in need of propitiation in this stormy place (as at the Alpis Graiae summit of the Little St Bernard Pass),[81] possibly even associated with much earlier megalith culture circa third millennium BCE as in the so-called "Hannibal Cromlech" there. When the Romans began describing this locus it was known as Poenina from Polybius onward as a montane pass region.[82] As noted in chapter 4, this became a sacred area complete with a small (11 by 7 meters) temple to Jupiter Poeninus in the early Flavian period, presumably under Vespasian, when the pass itself became known as Summus Poeninus [83] or highest part of the Pennine pass area, reflecting its Celtic roots.

The temple was built to abut into a jutting sacred rock (*roche sacré*) landmark where the Salassi Celts celebrated both solar religion with an added solar column (possibly predated by megalith calendrical monuments) also associated with Penn is highly likely; it is the intervening time between Polybius in the second century BCE and the Flavian temple that is nearly impossible to reconstruct, although Julius Caesar also references *Summus Poeninus* (emphasizing the need for Roman control) along with Strabo's and Tacitus' mentioning of the pass.[84]

The builders could have placed the temple nearly anywhere on the pass; that it was constructed to tie into the Celtic rock landmark had to be deliberate. Even the local stone employed for the temple was sacred as it derived from a very high quarry visible in the snowy peaks surrounding the site, the obvious higher locus where the storm god resided. [85]

LIKELY ALPINE PASS CONTEXTS WHERE CELTIC OR EARLIER
CULTURES HAD SOLAR COLUMNS OR HIGH ALTITUDE SHRINES

| General Alps | Pass Location | Altitude m |
|---|---|---|
| Pennine Alps | Grand-St-Bernard Pass | 2472 meters |
| Graian Alps | Petite-St-Bernard Pass | 2188 meters |
| Raetian Alps | Julier Pass | 2284 meters |
| Cunus Aureus | Splügen Pass | 2113 meters |
| Cottian Alps | Mont Cenis Pass | 2081 meters |

(Listed in order of probability. Sources: W.W. Hyde & P. Hunt)

**26. ALPINE GALLO-ROMAN TEMPLE, MARTIGNY**

*Architecture*

Architecture with combined Gallo-Roman elements is not easily reconstructed. Other than the Gallo-Roman temple in Martigny with its stone foundations intact, evaluating architectural remains in the region is difficult. Wiblé – the most authoritative archaeologist on Gallo-Roman material culture in the upper Rhone – excavated and published the first-century BCE Gallo-Roman square temple (*fanum*) to "Mercury" in Martigny (ancient Octodurus) of the mostly Veragri and partly Seduni tribes alongside the Rhone, discovered in 1976. In addition to bronze statuettes of the Celtic god Sucellus and another of a small Mercury, a huge repository of votive coins (at least 500 offered to the god of commerce) has been excavated around the temple whose architecture adapts

Gallic features to Roman structures and ritual. Its two-storey plan (cella with an upper floor gallery supported by columns) was a quadrangular podium with a square cella about 13 meters square (Figure 26). The fascinating bronze triple-horned Bull of Martigny associated with Jupiter also shows this mixing of Gallo-Roman elements, especially with the triplicity often emphasized in Celtic religion.[86] An inscription from St-Maurice (north of Martigny along the Rhone about 15 km) celebrates the unknown *Deus Sedatus*. Close by at Massongex (Gallo-Roman *Tarnaiae*), an inscription to *Iuppiter Optimus Maximus* is adjoined to *Taranis*, Celtic sky god whose name is the eponym for the locus of ancient *Tarnaiae*.[87]

**27. ALPINE GALLO-ROMAN 'BARN'**

Descriptions of Celtic structures may be helpful – mostly wood huts, as Livy noted – but there may be extant traditions still used today that have been in continuity for many centuries or even longer, such as the venerable Valaisian larch wood granaries and small barns (Figure 27) set up on rock foundations or piers. The timber log walls are larch planks joined by mortise and tenon and covered with schist roofs that are a hallmark of the mountain hamlets. Others have also noted the continuity of such traditional construction methods for such structures going back to the Late Iron Age in the Celtic or Gallo-Roman style now referred to as *casa retica* in current Italian contexts. [88] In related cases in the French Alps the mortised-and-tenoned wooden plank barn-like square structures are called *la fuste* (singular) in French when they are second levels over stone foundations (the lower stone rooms have served as livestock stables

81

even into the 20th century, said to have "animal heating"). Existing barns often have late Medieval or Renaissance dates carved in the dark, aged wood. This nearly identical Gallo-Roman construction method has been well established in the Valais. [89]

To reduce access to the grain by rats, many of the small granary barns (often as little as 15 feet square) are on raised stone piers. These piers are manmade piles of flat schist stone usually with at least one so wide (up to 30 in.) on each of the four piers so that no rat could maneuver around it. Traditional structures like these are likely to have carried down through innumerable generations; whether or not they bear resemblance to Celtic structures is not known. Flat worked stones with center depressions similar to those stones on piers of the existing mountain barns have been found in our excavation trenches at Plan de Barasson at 90 cm depth, which might suggest continuity of such *la fuste* structures over millennia.

### *Numismatics*

In remote parts of the Roman provinces, it has been long suggested by Michael Crawford and others that older minted coins might circulate for a longer period of time than in urban, highly populated contexts where recall is a given with nearly every dynastic change. Why else would Celtic coins be circulating so long after the fact (several centuries) unless it was Celts who were using them?

In collaboration with Italian archaeologist Cinzia Joris of the Soprintendenza of Archaeology for the Valle da Aosta, we also excavated with an international team led by Joris on what was previously thought before 1999 to be Mansio II of the Plan de Jupiter in 2000, but possibly reinterpretable as a Roman metals workshop along the mountain road (*Via per Alpis Poenina*). One bronze coin was found in a schist niche doorway threshold [Unit S-8] in beautiful condition. It was a 2nd c. BCE Sequani Gallic coin [Sequani # 5368] from Besançon and had a head on the obverse and stylized horse on the reverse.[90]

**28. ALPINE COINS ROMAN & GAULISH**

These Sequani (Seine river watershed source region) coin types in silver and bronze usually reproduce a recto abstract head derived from Greek (mostly) and Roman coins with verso abstract horse motif that might be evocative of Epona, the Celtic mare goddess worshipped as a horse deity (Figure 28, note Hadrianic period c. 135 CE silvered bronze coin as well).

Whenever the local La Tène B (after 300 BCE) culture transitioned from barter exchange systems to weights and measures with weight-determined metals, dates unable to know exactly, it is clearly under the influence of Classical minting and has the practical advantages of reifying value in a process not requiring the presence of actual objects exchanged but only small tokens thereof.

Where before, precious metals were primarily worn as jewelry or adornment, suddenly in the middle La Tène period, the Celts – in contact with Mediterranean Greeks and Romans from Massilia (Marseilles) to the Paduana - begin this important step toward abstraction in a change as much determined by practicality as well as status and imitative considerations.[91]

*Ceramics*

Gallo-Roman ceramics are by their very nature hybridized versions or imitations of individual Celtic and Roman types [92] as is fairly obvious to any archaeologist conducting research in the Alps in the periods from second century BCE to fifth century CE.

**29. STAMPED ROMAN TEGULAE**

Perhaps the most important chronometric finds between 1997-2005 in our Valais excavations are a total of over 24 stamped roof tiles (*tegulae*) all found in fragmentary form in Sondages D-E-F, between 18-102 cm in depth (Figure 29). Due to the datable stamps of the local roof tile manufacturers [*fabricatores tegulae*] Seppi, Publice, Saturnius and others who were active in the middle of the 1st c. CE in the area of Aosta (ancient *Augusta Praetoria*),[93] these date the initial structure roof to a *terminus post quem* in the middle and second half of the 1st c. CE and are thus integral to chronology of the structure on the site.  They are as follows:

- SEP[PI]   stamp mark of Seppi  (2 x)
- [SE]PPI   stamp mark of Seppi  (3 x)
- SEP[PI]   stamp mark of Seppi  (4 x)
- SE[PPI]   stamp mark of Seppi  (2 x)
- SEPP[I]   stamp mark of Seppi ?
- P F   stamp mark in ansata form:  P_____ F[ecit]
- F  stamp mark in ansata form:   ___ F[ecit]
- SATYR[N]  stamp mark of Saturnius, another local tegula fabricator (2 x)
- SATYRN    stamp mark of Saturnius
- PUB[LICE]   stamp mark of Publice, another local tegula fabricator
- PUBLI[CE]   stamp mark of Publice  (2 x)
- PUBL[ICE]  stamp mark of Publice   (2 x)
- C  CASS[IUS]  stamp mark of Caius Cassius, another local tegula fabricator

Of the 24 stamped tegulae, these 6 known *fabricatores* were, as mentioned, from Augusta Praetoria in the middle to late first century CE.  There is no guarantee that any of these named *fabricatores* are actually Roman, but aside from SEPPI the names have either been Romanized or bear likely Latinized inflections.

|    |              |
|----|--------------|
| 11 | SEPPI        |
| 5  | PVBLICE      |
| 3  | SATVRNIUS    |
| 2  | ARSENIVS     |
| 1  | P VALERIANVS |
| 1  | C CASSIUS    |

Unknown but likely same period (if structure dating is contiguous):

1      P F

1      ST P

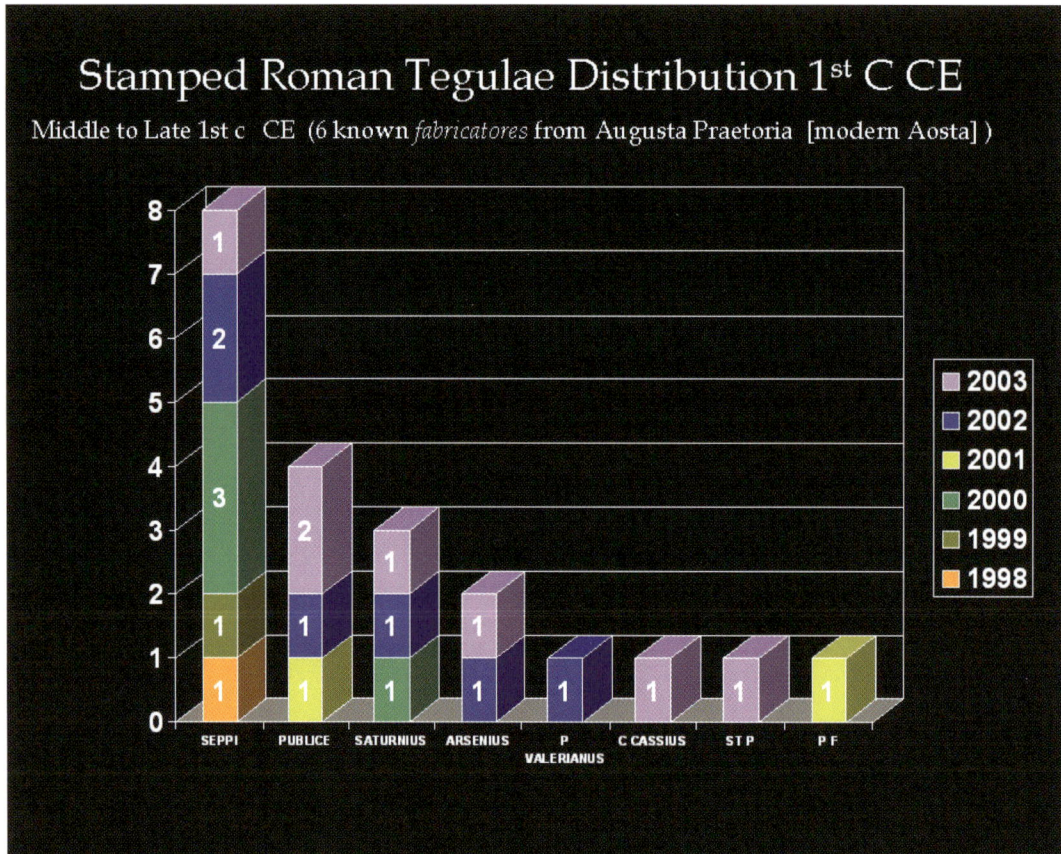

30. STAMPED TEGULAE DISTRIBUTION

All the roof tiles here are of a terra rossa fabric with a micaceous or phyllite temper traceable to the Dora Balthea river system that dissects Aosta to the south. The following tegulae were excavated in the 2003 season alone:

| Epigraphy | Name | Recorded Find | | Comment |
|-----------|------|--------------|---|---------|
| SEP[PI] | SEPPI | GSB-03.2179 | C-93 | |
| SATVRN[IVS] | SATURNIUS | GSB-03.2178a | C-64 | |
| PVB[LICE] | PUBLICE | GSB-03.2027 | C-69 | |
| PUBL[ICE] | PUBLICE | GSB-03.2069 | C-102 | ansata form |
| ARS[ENIUS] | ARSENIUS | GSB-03.2178b | C-72 | |
| ST P[-----] | ST P------ | GSB-03.2117 | C-96 | ansata form |
| C CASS[IUS] | CAIUS CASSIUS | GSB-03.2113 | C-97 | ansata form |

Perhaps the most interesting observation about the local tegulae (Figure 30) and their *fabricatores* is that the most prolifically represented *fabricator tegulae* is SEPPI, all the more important because this name is not Roman. According to Wiblé, SEPPI is most likely a local Salassi (Celtic) tribal name. On the one hand, it would stand to reason that, despite earlier conquest and enslavement by the Roman general Terentius Murro in 25 BCE in the Battle of Aosta, a local Salassi eventually had a concession for producing roof tiles by the mid-first century CE, but when Roman or Romanized names are also present among the other *fabricatores*, it might be an indicator of the cheapest or closest source or the possibility that he was the highest volume roof tile producer or that our sampling is not representative. The *ansata* (triangular handle) form of a *tabula ansata* is difficult to trace other than becoming important in the Augustan era and continuing throughout the Antonine period and beyond at least into the Paleo-Christian era (e.g, the 4th-6th century cemetery at Nemausus-Alyscamps, Nime, Provence), and may best be understood as representing quintessential "Roman-ness", although this is not fully established. The fact that some of our tegulae have the same name (Publice) both with and without the ansata stamp might suggest anything from different individuals with the same name (least likely), attempting to curry favor with Roman quaestors or other magistrates by making certain *fabricatores tegulae* more attractive or perhaps acquired Roman citizenship in the interim (more likely).

*Major Ceramic finds* [94] *(in addition to Tegulae)*

*Roman ceramic material* [95] (e.g., see Figure 31)

- 4 *mortarium* rim and base pieces, all from the same mortarium  [Sondage D - unit 4, depth 28-38 cm].

- other *mortaria* pieces, including a base, coiled or raised [Sondage E - unit 2 north, depth 26 cm], possibly the Aostan variety

- "pine cone" decorated lamp fragments [Sondage E- unit 2 north, depth 22 cm].

- both *Coupé Sable* (from Lugdunum) along with its "local" imitation Vindonissa fine ware fragments (see below), including rims and bases, generally less than 3-4 mm thickness [Sondage D - units 3/4/5, depths 18-37 cm].

- very numerous fragmentary Gallo-Roman cuisine and other fragments (over 3500 potsherds

- one lip / rim fragment of black burnished ware [Sondage D - unit 3, 33 cm depth].

- several transport amphorae fragments (insufficiently identifiable as to Dressel type]

- *lamp fragments* (from Bailey's 1980 indices / Leibundgut Types XV, XXIII, XXXV) [96] plus local Gallo-Roman lamp types.

*Gallo-Roman Ceramics: 1st century BCE to 2nd century CE* [97]  (e.g., see Figure 32)

## Roman Ceramics

Lamps

F5
- 80cm

Mortarium
Rim

**31. ROMAN CERAMICS**

- Black Vindonissa Ware ("local" copy of *coupé sable*)

- Red Carinated Ware (Lamboglia 5) late Terra Sigillata

- numerous imitation Arretine red ware ceramic fragments, including a dinner plate fragment of *terra sigillata* [Sondage D - units 2-5, depth range 18 - 57 cm] possibly from the Paduana southeast of Eporedia (modern Ivrea) outside the Val d'Aosta.

- numerous Barbotine ware and other decorated fragments, including incised circles and rings   [Sondage D - units 2-4, depth range 18- 57 cm].

- Gallo-Roman Gray cooking ware (great bulk of the fragmentary finds at 3500 ± pieces), coarse bodied and thick-walled [usually up to 1 cm thickness], often diagnostic in lips, rims and bases [Sondage D & E, all units, depth range 18-57 cm].

Thus, one tentative conclusion derived from the ceramic artifact material is that while a portion of the finds are Roman production pieces from standard Roman types (under 22%) imported to the area, the bulk of the Plan de Barasson site ceramics suggests a hybridized Gallo-Roman population because so much (greater than 78%) of the excavated ceramics to date are identifiable as Gallo-Roman production. The density of Gallo-Roman ceramics increases the further one moves away from the Roman road. This suggests that "Romanness" is only a superficial veneer in this remote area.

The caveat, however, is that local Romans (most likely a small minority population of around 25% even in the late first century CE) may have used Gallo-Roman material (e.g., Figure 32) because of its economic and numerical availability just as Romanized Gauls may have used imported Roman production ceramics for status or other reasons.

It is important to note that these ceramic finds presented here are excavated from remnants of a structure with a roof of Roman *tegulae* and *umbrices,* many of the former stamped.

The other nagging question is how representative can one fairly remote alpine site be? To date there is little to no statistical validity derivable from either any one site or together as an ensemble collection.

**Gallo-Roman Ceramics:
Carinated Ware (Lamboglio 5)**

**32. GALLO-ROMAN CERAMICS**

The recent work of Patrizia Framarin and Cinzia Joris on the Plan de Jupiter (Interreg III 2000 onward) in the Grand-St-Bernard Pass identifies many local Gallo-Roman ceramic wares, including the Late Terra Sigillata carinated ware (Lamboglia 5 style) as well as Gallic Terra Sigillata and Gray Ware and examines them in comparison to available Roman pottery. [98]

*Tabulae ansatae*

**33. TABULA ANSATA**

The 50 votive *tabulae ansatae* – in whole or fragments - from the Grand-St-Bernard collection assembled from the Plan de Jupiter over at least three centuries (starting with Canon Murith around 1764) are well published already in Mommsen, Barocelli, *CIL*, Walser, and most recently (2002) by this author. [99] While almost all evidence dedication to Jupiter, some with *I.O.M. (Iovi Optimo Maximo)* alongside *Poenino*, the majority (30 out of 50 votive bronzes or about 60%) acknowledge *Poeninus* – the Romanized Celtic god - as most important in the string of names, epithets and titles, emphasizing local domain and hybridization over universal domain.[100] These hybridized bronze votives with triangular handles (Figure 33) were given as prayers or advance thanks for the arduous journey over the high mountains in inclement weather even in summer, since it can snow heavily any day of the year at this altitude, as stated from the outset of this book. The bronze votive tabulae were probably nailed to the presumably wooden temple door because they usually have holes at each end and occasionally iron nails were also found in situ through these holes. A very few of the tabulae are also in silver or gold and a few also in filiform shapes (leaf/branch) and occasionally found with other Celtic gods also named. To date, more bronze *tabulae ansatae* have been found at Summus Poeninus than any other known Roman site.

## Conclusions

While is still not easy to answer the question of defining what makes up a "Roman" population here, actual Romans by citizenship must have been more numerous and demographically representative at lower elevation cities like Forum Claudii Vallensium (Octodurus-Martigny) or Augusta Praetoria (Aosta), both at around 500 meters elevation between Alpine ranges and perhaps having up to 5000 inhabitants each. Quantifying the "Roman-ness" of the high mountain region between Forum Claudii Vallensium (Martigny) and Augusta Praetoria (Aosta) by examining the site material by itself is also not yet possible, although the overall common-sense assumption of likelihood best supports a hybridized population with a predominant Gaulish ethnicity at the higher elevations, which probably best explains the high percentage of Gallo-Roman ceramics.

Is it possible that the 50 hybridized *tabulae ansatae* alpine bronzes here, having survived abnormally due to the year-round low temperature (an annual average of less than 7 °C), suggest that the quantity is skewed upward for this site and are thus not at all representative for all Roman or Roman frontier sites? Might other examples have survived elsewhere in similar conditions? Survival of alpine materials is greatly enhanced by low temperature where normal long-term decomposition and oxidation are inhibited by low diffusion – even if a quantity of water is present, it is in a frozen state for nine months of the year. Alpine climate and altitude, with diminished oxygen for oxidation, tend to preserve metals and organic remains with lower corrosion/decomposition values.[101] Ötzi the 5300+ year old "Iceman" in the Otzal Alps found in 1991 between the Tyrol of Italy and Austria around 3300 meters in a glacial melt is a prime example of this altitude and climatic enhancement of surviving material culture.

# Plan de Barasson Stratigraphy

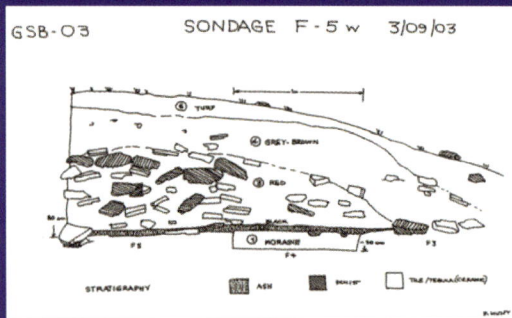

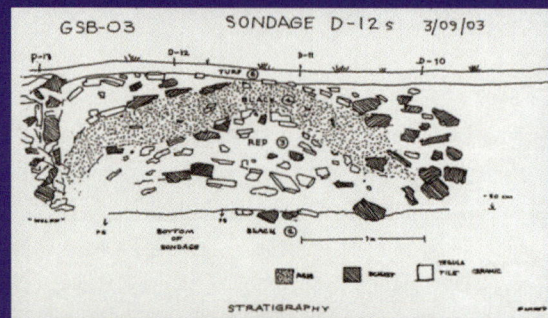

Sondage F-5

Sondage D-12

**34. PLAN DE BARASSON STRATIGRAPHY SLIDE**

Remote regions like the Alps may provide useful material evidences of definitive cultural hybridity for some of the reasons suggested. Kristiansen has used the phrase "buffer culture" for the Alps as a transitional or mixed local tradition in contrast to large regional traditions, just as might be expected during the period when neither Celtic or Roman cultures completely control this remote region of low population density, partly because the Romans preferred more hospitable climes and the local Gauls might also have thus enjoyed less Roman presence. Although the context in which Kristiansen poses the idea is not the time period considered here, he suggests elsewhere that natural divisions such as mountains may determine these buffer cultures. [102] While the cultural contact in the Alps between Celts and Romans may be generally comparable to many other such cultural contacts, the remoteness and arduous conditions present in the Grand-St-Bernard pass region that promote a Gallo-Roman culture may accentuate these transitional forms of cultural hybridity at the expense of Romanization. Our excavations (Figure 34) in the Grand-St-Bernard region since 1997 have not only shown periodic or possibly annual summer occupation of the area but also reinforced how important this Alpine route was for those needing to cross the high Alps for military, economic, religious and other reasons.

# Chapter Eight

## HANNIBAL IN THE ALPS: STANFORD ALPINE ARCHAEOLOGY 1994-2005

### Introduction

**35. HANNIBAL IN THE ALPS**

F. Walbank noted over a half century ago, "Few historical problems have so produced more unprofitable discussion than that of Hannibal's pass over the Alps."[103] While this is still true, the current Stanford Alpine Archaeology Project's most important ongoing research focus is on Hannibal in the Alps. Hannibal's famous passage through the Alps in 218 BCE (as interpreted in Figure 35) remains one of the most intrepid marches in history. Along with at least 25,000 soldiers, hundreds if not thousands of pack animals and scores of elephants, this surprising military maneuver was both bold and desperate and has inspired countless readers of ancient history in the intervening millennia.

Because it was undertaken in late fall – which is early winter in these high Alps – the Pleiades constellation could be easily viewed at a certain recorded point in the night sky, a journey that would have been daunting even in the summer became all the more dramatic. As Polybius wrote (*History* 3. 53-4):

> "After a journey of nine days, Hannibal gained the summit pass. He camped there and stayed for two days to rest the survivors of his army and wait for stragglers...As it was now almost the time for the setting of the Pleiades, snow had already settled on the summit...He noticed that his men were in a state of low morale for all that they had suffered and tried to cheer them up. He depended on the actual view of Italy, which lies so close under these mountains that when they are seen together, the Alps stand to Italy in the same way a citadel does to a city...He restored their spirits by showing them the plain of the Po..."

Unfortunately, the specific name of the pass Hannibal used was never mentioned in any ancient sources. Nor was it presumably mentioned by the informant, who may never have known its Celtic name anyway. Some of the Celts aided Hannibal and his Punic and mercenary army with guides and provisions; others were hostile and some may have tried to lead him into an Alpine trap, from which he escaped by clever resources and brave fortitude at some expense of men, animals and supplies to the surprise of both Celts and Romans.

### Stanford Hannibal Expeditions since 1994

The Stanford Alpine Archaeology Project has tracked Hannibal since 1994 across many passes (for example the Clapier-Savine as in Figure 36), using near contemporary sources like Polybius (*History*, Book 3) [104] in the mid-second c. BCE who claimed his informant's account was directly compiled from one of Hannibal's veterans who would have been very young during the march, and Livy (*History* XXI-XXXIX) who used Polybius and other possible sources nearly two centuries later. I refer herein mainly to Polybius because Livy often appears mostly derivative of Polybius, with more descriptive language but without more ample topography as his is so far after the fact where Polybius seems to have possibly known this landscape. On the other hand, Livy adds some accurate comments about the improbability of some of the often-suggested northern Hannibal routes such as the Grand-St-Bernard pass then known as Poeninus. Because this Poenine alpine region is one with which our Stanford project has spent considerable time, we concur with Livy on this (XXI.38), because as he notes this was Salassi territory,

**36. SAVINE DENTS D'AMBIN**

not Taurini. Additionally, this route would have added far too many days to Hannibal's journey being so far northward and requiring Hannibal to travel all the way around Lac Leman (Lake Geneva) likely from Geneva, adding far more than 600 stades distance up the Rhone almost regardless of where his army crossed, possibly with another 900-1000 stades and at least a week more total time in passage, which is negated by Polybius and Livy both agreeing on a nine day journey from the Rhone crossing to the Taurini.

Our Stanford team has hiked over at least 15 Alpine passes, many on multiple occasions, and compared their present landmark features to the topographic details given in Polybius and Livy. Allowing for a modicum of some erosional and geomorphological change, it is still possible to find a few favorable candidates among the western Alpine passes (now between France and Italy) and at the same time eliminate many more passes as unsuitable based on the ancient historians' narratives. Naturally, this also rests on several assumptions: that the informants of Polybius and others were accurate observers and honest in their recollections and that Hannibal himself was fairly well-informed (when not misinformed by Celts) and honest with his soldiers when he is reported to have made geographical statements. Previous studies include those of Torr (1925),[105] Lavis-Trafford (1956),[106] de Beer (1955, 1969),[107] Walbank (1956),[108] Meyer (1964),[109] Bradford (1981)[110] and many others, including fairly recent studies by Prevas (1998) and Lancel (1999).[111]

One of the best fairly modern and applicable analyses of the potential Hannibal passes comes from John Hoyte, whose 1958-9 Cambridge University expedition and resulting book *Alpine Elephant: In Hannibal's Tracks* (1960, repr. 1975) remains one of the most concise but logical examinations of the Western Alps. Hoyte's conclusions, shared by many today, include that the Col de Clapier is the best choice for Hannibal's passage for many reasons.

### Historic Suggested Hannibal Passes

Our Stanford team has made the passage several times over the Col de Clapier on foot and find it compelling as Hannibal's pass if one accepts the above assumptions, which is reasonable. Our first venture was in 1996 and our second in 2004, and we have approached it from both sides other times without crossing in 1995 and 1997 and we have also examined many passes in the Cottian Alps, Alpes Maritimes and Graian Alps in 1995, 1997, 1998, 1999, 2001, 2002 and 2005, including the Col du Mont Cenis, Col du Mont Genèvre, Col du Petit-St-Bernard, Col du Larche-Maddalena, among many others. Although several northern candidates have been raised at times, it is extremely unlikely that the Col du Grand-St-Bernard, Col du Fenêtre de Ferret and those passes eastward (Simplon, etc.) although we have also crossed them on foot many times comparing them to historic sources as well. The Cottian Alps, centrally located between France and Italy, appear to have the most likely candidates, but like Hoyte, we have eliminated most of them based on multiple conditions they do not meet.

100

## Hannibal Pass Criteria

Hoyte's conditions (also suggested elsewhere, but not as succinctly) include the following for Hannibal's pass.

1) It must be a distance of nine days away eastward by marching from the *Skaras* ("Island"), probably a fording place near a river confluence, after turning east at the Rhone ("Rhodanus") at a place which was 600 stades north from the Rhone mouth area. A stade is 200 meters, so 200 meters multiplied by 600 equals 120 km northward from the general area of the Rhone mouth, which, measuring from Tarascon, is very close (around 125-130 km) to where the Isere river (Isara in antiquity?) meets the Rhone today just north of Valence. It also makes sense to not measure from ancient Massilia (modern Marseilles) at the direct Rhone mouth because this city would have been mostly hostile and Hannibal would have most likely completely cicrumvented it in a northward direction. Thus measuring from around Tarascon (about 25 kms north of the Rhone's present Mediterranean junction from the Etang de Vaccares) is sensible as there is some consensus among geographers, especially geomorphologists, that the present Rhone mouth is considerably further south than in 200 BCE due to several millennia of alluviation. Hannibal would have probably crossed just south of the Rhone-Isere confluence because it marked hostile Allobroges territory, and the fording here would have been shallower in the fall than in the spring during heavy snowmelt runoff.

37. BRAMANS 'BARE ROCK' PLACE

2) Hannibal's pass must have a deep gorge and cliffs for Celtic ambush (its summit must be one day's march from "bare rock" (*leukopetron* in Greek) assault). There is such a cliff and bare rock ravine (Figure 37) just east of Bramans and west of Le Planey en route to Clapier at the day's journey mark.

3) It must be broad enough at its general summit to support an army camp of thousands of soldiers and animals, with foraging grass or pasture even in October. Clapier presently pastures cattle in summer at 8000 feet in the wide Savine valley even at its western summit (Figure 38).

**38. CLAPIER-SAVINE CATTLE AT 8000 FEET**

4) It must be high enough to have some permanent snow on its passage in October or remnant snow from the previous year on its steep Italian side (eastern flank) where elephants and men slipped on the descent as Polybius related (*Hist.* 3.55). This permanent snowline threshold is usually around 8,200 ft. (approximately 2,470 meters) altitude, although this can vary from year to year (Figure 39). We have encountered such snow even in a very hot year (2004) but not in every year (2006).

5) There should be several glacial tarn-like natural lakes or a high volume of water even in October on the western (France) summit approach for the water consumption needs of pack animals, including elephants, which consume many liters per diem. Today Clapier has several such lakes, including Lac de Savine, which seems to have merged several smaller lakes by alluviation.

**39. CLAPIER SUMMIT SNOW – 8200 FEET**

6) It must have a dangerous, very steep descent into Italy. Clapier has an incredible descent, over 4000 feet at a gradient of close to 70% in places.

7) It must look down into Italy "from the fortress walls" eastward to the Paduana (Po River valley), as Hannibal reputedly brought his exhausted army to a place at the summit and told his men to look down into the Paduana and the hinterlands of Roman Italy to revive their spirits. It is easy to see the Po river valley and Torino from just below the Italian summit of Clapier (Figure 40).

8) It must be three days march to the Taurini tribe center (present-day Torino). Clapier is also a two and a half day walking distance for an army after a half-day's steep descent and rest. To these prior conditions, I add the following condition.

9) Its western approach should be situated on the margins of the hostile Allobroges tribe territory as these enemy Celts barred Hannibal from passage further north. The present Isere river fork on the Rhone has traditionally marked this ancient territory, something that not many prior studies have fully addressed. Others have argued against the idea of the Allobrogres as not being so sedentary, but rivers have historically marked natural boundaries - just as Polybius stated some hostile Celtic tribes massed along riverbanks - and the Allobroges would have themselves faced the traditional territory of tribes like the Ucenni on the south side of the Isere. The naming of the Allobroges as both barring the way north and attacking on the eastward alpine ascent in Polybius (*Hist*. 3.50, 52) argues strongly for a Cottian Alps passage where the Isere (Isara in antiquity) and Arc rivers are its watershed. According to the *Tabula Imperii Romani*, the Val d'Arc watershed became the territory of the Medulli soon after it

merged with the Val d'Isere (today not far from St-Jean de Maurienne), so these Medulli might have been some of the "other tribes" hostile to Hannibal's army mentioned by Polybius (*Hist* 3.53-54) as he neared the pass.

### Why Col de Clapier is best to date

To date, only the Col du Clapier (and its immediately adjacent Savine-Coche pathway) best fulfill all these conditions in my opinion, shared with John Hoyte and Serge Lancel, among others. Most of the other historically long-favored candidates are either too low around 6,000-7000 ft (about 1700-2200 meters altitude) - including Mont Genèvre, Mont-Cenis (and Petite-Mont-Cenis), Petite-St-Bernard - to have old snow from a past winter as Polybius noted

**40. CLAPIER SUMMIT, TURIN VIEW**

when the descending elephants broke through fresh snow and slipped on ice from the previous winter. In addition, they do not have a view eastward to the Paduana (the same three mentioned) or are also too far south to be near the Taurini upon descent (Col du Larche-Maddalena, Col du Tende) as well as too low or are too far north to be 600 stades from of the Rhone mouth (Grand-St-Bernard, Fenêtre du Ferret). They also do not debouche toward the Taurini or have little to no pasturage and space to accommodate an army at their summit and too high for elephants altogether (Col du Traversette, favored by Gavin de Beer in 1952 and Prevas in 1998). A few other passes might be possible that have not yet been considered rising from the Val Cenis close to Col du Clapier, itself part of the Arc river watershed that drains into the Isere and then

104

into the Rhone westward. Furthermore, only the Mont-Cenis and Petit-St-Bernard, along with Clapier, begin in the west in Allobroges territory. Also an excellent possible Col de Clapier side route is the directly-adjacent Col de Savine-Coche, which shares its meeting of conditions extrapolated from Polybius. The Savine-Coche route, favored by Lavis-Trafford in 1943 and Lancel more recently in 1999, which path we also followed in 1996, only veers from the Clapier route in the last few hundred meters from the summit. Prevas believes the much higher Traversette is a better candidate with an incredible view of the Paduana, although I believe Clapier's view into the Po river valley is also magnificent along the summit ridge, and looks east to Turin just a few meters below the summit. Our 1996 team found ample snow while passing over during an August snowstorm and our 2004 August team found plenty of snow just on the immediate descent as well after a sunny passage, as mentioned (and already shown in Figure 39). I understand why Prevas claims Petite-Mont-Cenis would have been easier and thus better, in his estimate eliminating Clapier, which is true today. I have great reservations, however, against rejecting Clapier only on this basis. First, I would suggest the more accessible but lower Petite-Mont-Cenis en route and adjacent to Clapier could have been easily guarded by hostile Celts (Medulli, Graioceli or other local tribes) or their duplicitous guides, who compelled his journey into what they hoped would be a trap. But Hannibal escaped this trap by descending a near impossible route. Second, Hannibal or his scouts would need to have known about the narrower Petite-Mont-Cenis route, which is not at all visible from the valley floor or even clear from the ridge that the present footpath follows (even assuming Hannibal's passage traveled this particular footpath). Third, the narrow Petite-Mont-Cenis path also veers due north first whereas the broader Clapier route travels eastward, the direction Hannibal and his scouts would be expecting and needing. Our Stanford team has hiked this pathway from Le Planey multiple times and the Petite-Mont-Cenis route is not at all obvious.

Going back to Livy, who suggested the Druentia river watershed for Hannibal's passage (XXI.32) - often debated as either the Durance or the Drome rivers - all the passes (including the Mont-Genèvre, Argentières, Larche-Maddalena and Traversette) leading up the Durance river watershed start at too southerly a position since they do not begin at a 600 stades (120 km) distance from the Rhone mouth, but rather only about 60 km maximum distance to where the Durance meets the Rhone. If on the other hand, Hannibal's army crossed between the Durance and the Isere rivers or in the region of the Drome and went due east, the army would have had to negotiate two high alpine passes, not one, and neither Polybius or Livy hint at this, let alone make any such assertion. Even though many historians, including Niebuhr and Mommsen in previous centuries, had traditionally favored the Petite-St-Bernard pass, not only is it too low at under 7200 ft and it does not descend east into the Paduana with any such view since it faces north, but it also descends like the Grand-St-Bernard into the Val d'Aosta, and thus not into the Taurini tribe territory but the Salassi and is furthermore a much longer journey than Hannibal would have taken with about a week of added journeying days required.

*Conclusions*

Under these considerations (and the compounded probabilities of matching up with all the requisites), the dramatic Col du Clapier with its superb Paduana view and steep descent (Figure 41) is becoming more accepted as the likeliest pass to date used by Hannibal and his army with elephants. The Stanford Alpine Archaeology project surveyed this pass again on foot in 2006 along with a few other passes in the Cottian Alps, including Traversette. Our continuing objectives in 2007-2008 and beyond will be also include surveying for possible macro or micro scale surface features such as tumuli that an army camp might have left behind on the permanent landscape. To date, no elephant remains (except prehistoric mastodon-mammoth) or contemporary Celtic coins have been found in the Val d'Arc watershed in any proximity to the region, but they have not been found in any other alpine context either. In view of all the conditions met, Col de Clapier and the immediately adjacent Savine-Coche (essentially the same pass a few hundred meters on the south side of the Savine valley but with a better view of the Taurini and an even more dangerous descent) remain the best candidates for

Hannibal's Alpine passage. On the other hand, until absolutely datable and identifiably Carthaginian or Numidian victims of the legendary passage - possibly including elephant bones - are reliably found in context, locating Hannibal's Alpine pass remains an academic guesswork problem. Our Stanford team will consider the Clapier route and several other Alpine passes again on foot in coming field seasons from 2007 onward, hoping to add more definition to the question or even its possible answer.

**41. CLAPIER DESCENT (VIEW WEST) FOLLOW UPPER RIGHT TO LOWER CENTER**

# Chapter Nine

## HANNIBAL EXPEDITION: 2006 FIELD SEASON

### Introduction

As noted, in August 2006 the Stanford Alpine Archaeology Project continued its focused search for Hannibal's pass crossed in 218 BCE. The Stanford group of 16 students and staff traveled at least 3500 kms through the Alps following the Isere-Arc river watersheds, the Durance-Queyras watersheds and the Dora Balthea and Rhone watersheds. Since the outset of our research in 1994-96, we have had ongoing assistance from John Hoyte, co-leader of the Cambridge Alpine Elephant Expedition 1958-59 [112] as well as more recent collaboration (2006) with John Prevas, fellow explorer and military historian-author.[113]

While some of our 2006 alpine routes were by vehicle over the Mont-Genèvre (see Figure 42, green on the major Hannibal routes picture)), the Mont-Cenis (blue), the Little St. Bernard (turquoise) and others, our primary exploration over the passes was hiking on foot.

Passes covered on foot included the Great St. Bernard (gold), from below Bourg-St-Pierre to the summit, 5000 – 8300 - 7500 ft, crossing from Switzerland into Italy (around 20 kms), the Fenêtre de Ferret (also gold) (7000 – 9000 - 7000 ft) crossing from Italy to Switzerland and back to Italy (around 10 kms), among others, but we especially concentrated on the Col du Clapier (red) (4000 – 8600 – 3000 ft.) from Bramans and Le Planey in France to the Susa Valley in Italy (around 30 kms) and the Col de la Traversette (yellow) (6000 – 9600 – 6000 ft.) from France to the border of Italy (around 10 kms). In all, our Hannibal searches in summer of 2006 covered at least around 20,000 vertical feet by hiking around 80 kms.

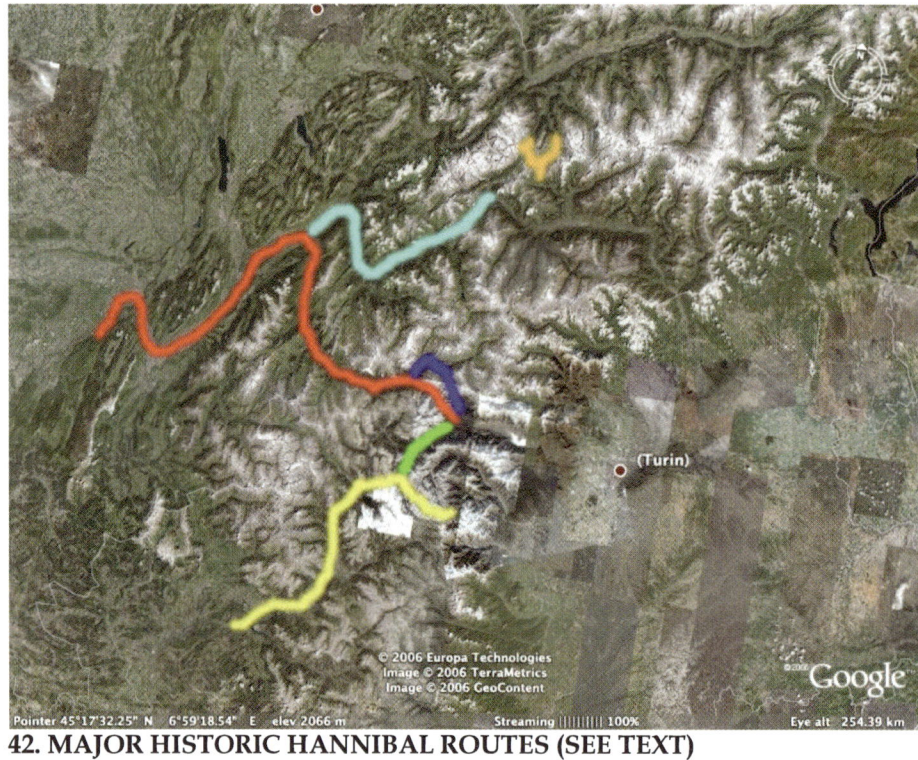

**42. MAJOR HISTORIC HANNIBAL ROUTES (SEE TEXT)**

*Traversette Route – Queyras Gorge*

We closely examined the Queyras river gorge between Abriès and Ristolas all the way to its confluence with the Durance River, looking for potential ambush sites that fit with the accounts of Polybius and Livy where hostile Celts made passage difficult. We also closely examined the Arc river for potential ambush sites in gorges (Polybius III.52.8), especially the gorges between just below Bramans to Fort Esseillon and to Modane, and followed the Arc from near Grenoble to Lanslebourg. Additionally we followed the Isere River from its Arc confluence northeast all the way to the Little St. Bernard and the Durance River from below the Queyras confluence all the way northeast to Mont-Genèvre, Clavieres, Oulx and Susa.

## Saint Bernard Routes (Grand and Petite)

While both the Great St Bernard (Pennine Alps) and Little St. Bernard (Graian Alps) are not optimum for matching with the best ancient sources (Polybius and Livy), some traditions, even in antiquity, considered them as potential Hannibal routes, and some ancient sources have posited that Poeninus derived from "Punic" due to association with Hannibal's march, but this view was not even held by Livy (*Hist.* XXI.38), because as he noted this was Salassi territory, not Taurini. Nonetheless, we have marched on foot on occasion to verify that both of these passes would add far too many more days than the nine days (or possibly fifteen according to how we read Polybius) to Hannibal's journey. A conservative estimate would take Hannibal's force at least three weeks to cover the greater distance required to pass through Salassi territory. More important, Hannibal would not end up anywhere near Torino (Taurini tribal heartland still named by this toponym) but instead much further to the northeast near Ivrea just outside the Val d'Aosta and would then take another possible week to march back west, which would be most unlikely as he then headed further southeast.

## Clapier Route through Arc River Watershed

We also confirmed from the top of the Clapier – especially to the right at the 8400 ft elevation summit directly above and south of the present pass path – that the plain of the Po and Paduana and even Turin itself can be easily seen as if from the relative position of the so-called "citadel" or "lofty summit" (*'akropoleos*) of the Alps to the plain of Italy as Polybius states (*Histories* III.54.2-3). That the exact region of Turin was the putative location of the Taurini tribe around 200 BCE (into whose tribal territory Hannibal directly descended (*Hist.* III.60.8: "Taurini who lived at the foot of the mountains") is difficult to argue against, as we have maintained elsewhere, as Clapier is much closer to the traditional center of the Taurini region (present-day Turin itself) than any other pass, especially in contrast to Traversette.

**43. BRAMANS GORGE (*LEUKOPETRON*)**

Our tentative conclusions were that the Arc river watershed best fit the ambush and journey conditions set forth by Polybius and Livy, especially the gorge between Modane-Fort Esseillon and Bramans. Additionally, the "bare rock" (Figure 43) or more specifically "white rock" (*leukopetron* in Polybius *Histories* III.53.5) place as the overnight site (Ruisseau d'Ambin-Bramans gorge) of half of Hannibal's army one day from the summit of Col de Clapier best fit in our estimation the topographical conditions set forth by Polybius. This was made more plausible by the nature of the rock itself, because the huge eroded cliff here is of both dolomite and gypsum. While it was clear to our survey on foot that the Bramans gorge-Ruisseau d'Ambin is of fairly soluble rock whose outer surface and depth of erosion would not be the same as what Hannibal's army could have seen in 218 BCE – given the expected or assumed geomorphological change in the interim – nonetheless we could also see much older weathered rock of the

**44. BRAMANS GORGE GEOLOGY**

same geological exposures that would have existed around 2,224 years ago and would have merited this identical description of "bare rock" or more specifically "white rock" (*leukopetron*) for Polybius and Hannibal's passage. Traditional translations of this Polybius excerpt have rendered *leukopetron* as "bare rock" place but this is best translated as "white rock" and the geological nature of the very white gypsum and dolomite here above Bramans really establishes a strong possible identification for this locus. On the other hand, it is also possible that this literary passage could also be descriptive of fresh limestone or other unweathered white carbonate rock from recent avalanches, since many pale carbonates frequently weather in visible grays to blackish hues over time, a fact that would not make such a place stand out at present. We hiked up this Bramans canyon (following the stream Ruisseau d'Ambin) and noted that it would not only be an optimum Celtic ambush site at its narrow opening but its terminus would put Hannibal and his army with their proverbial backs to the wall while also providing protection because of steepness where the Celts would be unable to much disturb the Carthaginians and their allies. It was and is also wide enough at its eastern terminus in several hectares to accommodate a whole army inside, in this case half the army. The floor of this gorge, (Figure 44) however, has, like the sides of the gorge, gone through much erosion in the intervening several millennia and would thus be unlikely to yield much archaeological data even if Hannibal might have camped here "one day from the

113

summit" (Polybius III.53.5).  After hiking the potential Hannibal routes through the Alps for years, it appears to me that the *leukopetron* "white rock" geology of this dolomite and gypsum gorge (Figure 44) best fits the historical description of Polybius to date.


## Global climate relative to local paleoclimate

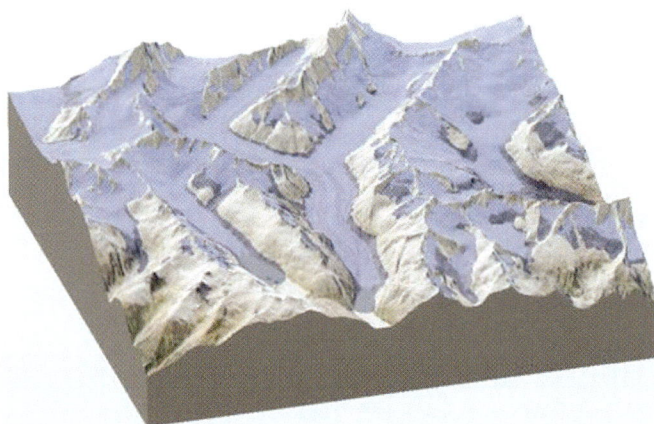

**45. SWISS GLACIERS IN 1850 – BERNESE OBERLAND**

Possibly due to global warming, we noticed for the first time in our observed experience, that neither Clapier - pathway at 2480 meters (8200 ft) but view above the path at 2540 (around 8400 ft) or Traversette at 2970 meters (nearly 10,000 ft) had much visible snow along the paths we hiked in August. The Ambin Glacier in the nearby Ambin valley adjacent but visible along the Clapier route has also lost most of its ice and snow in a ten year observed period between 1996-2006 (although enormous glacial recession has happened since 1850, for example relative to Figure 45).

Geomorphological evidence is mounting that the alpine landscape as a whole has changed considerably in the past several millennia, expanded below. This may partially explain why no surficial archaeological evidence of Hannibal's passage has yet been found. It also suggests that if Hannibal passed through Clapier, its relative stability compared to Traversette's instability slightly enhances a greater likelihood of ultimate archaeological success.

**46. ANCIENT SUSTEN PASS RECONSTRUCTED**

Ongoing alpine paleoclimatic research, at this point mostly theoretical, is based in part on relict ancient wood artifact finds trapped under receding glaciers between ice and moraine as found, for example, in the Susten pass in Switzerland, notably a considerable distance of over 150 kilometers away in a very different Alpine massif. Evidence suggests that 2000 years ago the tree line may have actually been considerably higher in places (up to 2700 meters elevation or possibly 700-900 meters higher) with less glaciation than in the last several millennia. Schlüchter and Jörin are with the Institut für Geologie, Universität Bern, and while their study is very theoretical and limited mostly to the Susten pass, [114] (Figures 46 & 47) it is likely to be more or less relatively applicable elsewhere in the Alps. On the other hand, the Cottian Alps are significantly further south and west and face not only different directions but also had different paleoclimates. Although it is yet unknown how to extrapolate and apply this as yet theoretical data elsewhere, as in the more southwestern Cottian Alps, the implications for Hannibal research are potentially profound. The likelihood of finding extant surficial ancient wood samples at

**47. MODERN SUSTEN PASS**

Clapier or Traversette passes as at Susten pass is extremely remote as there is no recent glacial recession uncovering such botanical remains, since at both Clapier and Traversette no known glacial activity has been historically recorded and no glacial recession is certainly presently visible as at Susten pass.

Until we have more geomorphological data, these paleoclimatic implications could go in several different directions. One possibility is that Traversette might have been far more accessible from both directions (French ascent and Italian descent) than at present if the visible glaciation postdates 218 BCE, which would enhance its Hannibal possibilities, but such late glaciation is extremely unlikely.

If the glaciation is later than 2500 years before present or contemporary with Hannibal, even more unlikely, its lower moraine - much reduced - would most likely have not provided the current flatter campground area near the Mont Viso hut visible in the last image in this report. Another possibility is that the highly erosive and narrow "window" of the pass itself may not have existed at all as at present without such glaciation.

If the glaciation predated and was finished (fully recessed) before 218 BCE but the erosive state of rock fall had not filled the glacial cirque as at present, Traversette would have been almost impossible to cross due to the steepness of the cirque bowl.

On the other hand, a different possibility is that Hannibal's passage through deep snowfall, as both John Prevas and Bruno Martin have personally verified to me in their experience at different times (most recently in June of this year), would have made the Traversette crossing much easier in 218 BCE than at present. The vertical steepness and elevation of the Traversette's ascent, however, shows enormous variability for change as the verticality (with a higher gravity-gradient determined potential energy stored up and then released as kinetic energy) make this pass very unstable over the past several millennia and probably longer.

*Erosional implications of Clapier relative to Traversette*

The erosional implications for Clapier appear more directed to its steep eastern Italian descent because it is a much more long term stable environment and a much broader, shallower ascent on its western French side through the Val Savine - itself also an old glacial valley - than the immediate area around the Traversette, whose last kilometer of ascent is very steep (in places with a gradient of up to 70% over 500 meters) whereas the Clapier ascent is not at all steep at the summit with a gradient of less than 5-10% over the last few kilometers. The descent on both the Traversette and on the Clapier can be greater than 70% over 500 meters especially after the first kilometer (since the eastern Alpine scarp is generally much steeper overall than the western face), but the Traversette descent is most difficult at the immediate summit – appearing suicidal to this archaeologist! - whereas the first leg of the Clapier descent is presently much shallower than the Traversette, easy at first within the first kilometer and then steepest over the next several kilometers (as can be seen in Figure 3 here). To date, in a more southerly context than the Susten pass in the Swiss Alps, the chronology of the ancient Traversette glaciation is best estimated as pre-218 BCE and thus pre-Hannibal, which would appear to make a Traversette Hannibal route much more problematic.

We have had very cordial assistance from our friend and colleague John Prevas regarding Col de la Traversette, who has answered very soundly the long-held criticism that there was no campground for an army at Traversette. After our topographical survey, we believe John Prevas is right in proving that a campground for an army could exist only an hour from the summit, although it would not have been possible for the whole army to have seen this a few minutes away, as is possible at Clapier where the Savine valley is literally a five minute walk and much more spacious in accommodating both view and army almost simultaneously. As I have stated elsewhere, many prior studies have pinpointed Clapier or Clapier-Savine Coche as the most likely Hannibal route, including those of Wilkinson and Dunbabin, [115] (although Goldsworthy scrupulously avoids any mention of the most likely pass by name [116]) also Hazel [117] as well as John Hoyte and most recently Serge Lancel. [118]

*Textual ambiguity about Hannibal's Rhone River crossing*

One of the difficulties in attempting to establish Hannibal's route from the Rhone valley is the uncertainty due to textual brevity about where he crossed the Rhone River. Many historians hold that he crossed in the south near Avignon, while many others maintain he crossed further north closer to Valence. Part of the problem lies in how many Greek *stades* (a *stade* is about 200 meters) his army is believed to have traveled after crossing the Rhone (600 stades or around 120 kms/80 mi.). Another part of the problem lies in how many other rivers he would have had to ford en route since only the Rhone crossing and possibly Isere crossings are recorded. If on a southerly route and he turned east fairly soon after crossing near Avignon and followed the Durance watershed, he would not have to cross another river until the Queyras gorge. If he crossed further north near Valence and followed and crossed the Isere and then the Arc watersheds, he would not have to cross another river until near Bramans or thereabouts. But if he crossed the Rhone river in the south near Avignon and continued north along the east bank, he would have to cross again at the Drome watershed - unless he turned southeast at this point and followed the Val Drome over to the Durance river- until reaching the Isere watershed.

One of the potential problems with the Val Drome-Durance route is that in October the army would have needed to cross an initial mountain range (1300-1700 meters elevation with only one possible 1100 meter gap) over the Drome river watershed and south into the Durance watershed that could have been sufficiently high and difficult to be considered alpine and certainly montane in itself, which crossing is not recorded in the ancient sources as the first of several mountain ranges. In fact, Hannibal is only recorded as having crossed only one entire range of mountains in Polybius and arriving at one summit (Polybius III.53.9). On the other hand, Livy's account is more ambiguous about the exact number of mountains crossed (although only one highest summit is common to both Polybius and Livy) and we should not dismiss Prevas' reading here or elsewhere, especially because Livy, right or wrong, also names the Druentia river as the route of Hannibal (Livy XXI.31.9), which can hardly be

118

any other than the Durance river. As mentioned in a previous chapter, two other factors suggesting more the northerly Isere route is the 600 stades distance he traveled up the Rhone (*Rhodanus*) and the Allobroges tribe hostility he encountered, which would have been unlikely so far to the south and whose territory is traditionally bordered near the Isere watershed. Naturally, one of the concerns facing historical study and topographical and geoarchaeological alpine reconstruction from the texts of Polybius and Livy is whether we are reading too much literality into these ancient texts.

### *Voreppe Oppidum: "Gateway to the Alps"?*

An excellent recent study (2006) by historian de Galbert in France [119] also supporting the Clapier route - suggests the ruins of a Celtic oppidum at Voreppe near and to the west of Grenoble that may closely match the topographic textual account of a Celtic attack by the hostile Allobroges tribe over controlling the narrowest point of the route (Figure 48) near where Hannibal's army may have passed. The logic of de Galbert here best fits the accounts of Polybius and Livy as this is the narrowest point (Polybius III.50.9-51-3) of the Isere (Isara?) river through which Hannibal would have passed if he came this route. According to de Galbert, Voreppe also matches Polybius' description of the "Gate to the Alps" or the strategic point where he encamped "at the foot" (*katastratopedeusas*) of the high places" (Polybius III.50.6) out of which the Isere river flows toward the Rhone plain, also mentioned in Livy as the "first slopes" (*primos...clivos*) (Livy XXI.32.8), easily associated with the Isere gap between the Chartreuse and Vercors massifs. This narrow gap is called the "Cluse de Voreppe", and the ruins of the likely oppidum there is a context our project hopes to assist in surveying and excavating in 2007-08 in an international collaborative project as we remain in continuing contact with de Galbert. While there have been prior archaeological surveys and even brief excavations at Clapier - particularly the Val Savine potential campground with a few sondage or sounding test pits between 1993-96 and in the past decade or so - there have never been extensive excavations on the Clapier-Savine Coche route and summit or at Traversette, certainly never by geoarchaeologists with training in alpine geomorphology. A geomorphology study by Mahaney et alia has also fairly recently considered Traversette,[120] but it is unknown if this is a comparative study with Clapier, in which case Clapier appears more likely based on geomorphological stability opposed to the original narrowness and modern fresh appearance of the approach to Traversette on the steep ascent, both suggestive of great instability through time.

**48. VOREPPE OPPIDUM (AT NARROWEST ISERE VALLEY POINT) UPPER LEFT**

*Conclusions*

These factors cited above still lead us to consider the Col du Clapier-Savine Coche route (Savine Coche is immediately adjacent by less than a kilometer at the summit) as the optimum candidate for Hannibal's march. Other concerns include the difficulties in establishing the history and date of Col de la Traversette from Hannibal's time. Assuming its relative topographic similarity in antiquity to the present, Traversette's highly-eroded glacial cirque (which if datable to before 218 BCE would most likely have been much steeper 2,224 years ago), its unstable cliffs, fresh rock fall on the ascent near the summit and extremely precipitous descent for the first 500 meters) are in contrast to the relative geomorphological stability of the Savine-Clapier route with its own precipitous descent. In addition, an ancient army could negotiate Traversette only under certain conditions and elephants might be impossible at Traversette unless both sides were under heavy snow to lessen the extreme steepness of the gradient. Even then, the path of thousands of soldiers, pack animals and elephants over Traversette's snow would render its passage very difficult on the ascent and suicidal on the descent. The more geologically stable Clapier ascent is congruent with Polybius and Livy) and Clapier's precipitous descent its dangerous enough and would have likely also decimated men and elephants alike on the descent. Much continuing research needs to be conducted at both Clapier and Traversette and other contexts, collaborative study with French and Italian archaeological colleagues as well as pioneering paleoclimatological research. John Prevas has rightly demonstrated and we agree that the Traversette cannot be so easily dismissed, yet Clapier-Savine Coche appears to best fit the topographic described by Polybius, the most careful of ancient historians.

# Chapter Ten

## HANNIBAL OR HASDRUBAL?

## SOME NUMISMATIC CONSIDERATIONS

### Introduction

What kind of archaeological evidence could distinguish two very similar events only a little more than a decade apart? Of all the possible absolute or relative chronometers an archaeologist might use, sometimes coins are the most datable artifacts. This is the optimum evidence our Stanford Alpine Archaeology project hopes to ultimately find in our ongoing Hannibal research expeditions. As Metcalf says, "The relationship between numismatics and archaeology has always been close...coin finds help to date strata or levels..." [121] Possibly applicable here, the well known and intrepid Hannibal Barca's crossing of the Alps was in 218 BC and his less well known brother Hasdrubal Barca followed him around 208-07 BC. Both traveled with an army and elephants; although Hasdrubal's was apparently a much smaller army and the second crossing happened during spring as opposed to Hannibal's passage in late fall moving into early winter.

According to Appian, circa 150 AD therefore late relative to Polybius and Livy, writes (*Roman History* VII.1.4), "Hannibal crossed into Gaul with 90,000 infantry soldiers, 12,000 cavalry, and 37 elephants." Many historians find all these numbers dubious, with too high a number for infantry and too low for elephants; rather that only 37 elephants survived the Alps. Appian also claims further on (VII.8.52) about Hasdrubal that "Hasdrubal debouched into Etruria with 48,000 infantry soldiers, 8,000 cavalry and 15 elephants." Again, to many scholars these numbers are also arguable, but for the sake of an archaeological argument, one of the optimum artifactual evidences that could separate the two events would be the numismatic evidence: coins from separate mintings.

## Alpine numismatic record to date

No such coins have been found or identified as such to date in any provable Alpine context, but all else being nearly the same other than relative size – Carthaginian and mixed (e.g. Numidian and Celtic allies among others) armies with culturally identifiable military gear, pack animals and elephants, etc, - the coin evidence if found could be very important in answering this question. Coins are often sufficient chronometers in archaeological arguments. We also know that Hannibal used coins as a "formidable tool of political propaganda." [122] Hannibal also must have paid some of his Celtic allies – including heavy Celtic cavalry [123] – or less hostile Celtic tribes en route for food and foraging rights in silver or bronze coin.

## Barcid Punic Mintings

**49. HANNIBAL SHEKEL C. 220 BCE**

Melqart was originally a patron deity of Phoenician Tyre but was transferred to Punic iconography and the Phoenicians apparently innovated the introduction of bronze into coins (long after gold, silver and electrum had already been utilized) but at first only to replace the smallest silver denominations as "small change". [124] That Melqart would appear on Phoenician imagery and subsequent Punic coins is logical given Punic myth and religion.

124

According to most accounts, Hannibal minted some silver and bronze coins in Spain around 220 BCE (e.g., Figure 49) just before his famous campaign into Italy - apparently minted from Carthagena shortly after its founding after mid-3rd c. BC.[125] - and while the Phoenician-Punic deity on the face of some silver AE shekel coins is usually suggested to be that of the myth heroic deity Melqart-Herakles, it is also maintained that Melqart wears Hannbal's features in this minting.[126] His brother Hasdrubal a little more than a decade later around 209 BC also apparently minted coins for his campaign and with what is most often also interpreted as Melqart but this

50. HASDRUBAL SHEKEL C. 210 BCE

time with Hasdrubal's features (Figure 50).[127] The coins have sufficiently different faces on their obverse sides as to understandably represent different persons, but this is not a certainty. The *post quem* and *ante quem* arguments implicit here, however, may make such dating distinctions possible.

If Hasdrubal also carried some of his brother's slightly earlier coins from around 220 BC on the circa 209 campaign, this melange could greatly complicate the matter unless both coin types were found in the same context, in which case the later date would be the logical *terminus post quem*, in other words the archaeological context could not be from Hannibal's campaign. On the other hand, if only the Hannibal minted coins were found in sufficient number (without any of Hasdrubal's), this would almost certainly be more evidential for Hannibal than for Hasdrubal but again not absolute. This numismatic and thus chronometrically valid distinction, however, could be useful regardless of whether the two brothers used the same or different passes.

That such bronze and silver coins and related bronze material can survive intact and even pristine in Alpine contexts is a given, underscored by the low temperature-low diffusion and minimal oxidation and thus good preservation factors exhibited in alpine coin finds that make them readily identifiable, as our Stanford Alpine Archaeology Project has experienced. [128] There may also be Numidian issues of Punic bronze coins after 208 BC in the Alps that could conceivably date around the end of Hasdrubal's alpine and Italian campaign. [129]


*Numismatic caveats*

Now, some of the added logical caveats must be addressed. Coins do not necessarily remain in circulation very long in urban contexts but in remote locations they may survive in circulation for many decades after being superseded by successive mintings. But the fact that they can and do circulate makes it difficult to know if any such theoretical coins were carried by either of these Carthaginian armies or by random Celts traveling through the alpine passes long after the events, either because coins were paid out to Celts or were scavenged after skirmishes from bodies, as most soldiers in an army would be likely to carry a few coins for contingencies. Any such coins could also survive in hoards, which would generally be more useful for statistical purposes to examine dating ratios of earlier to later coins, etc. Sadly to date, any of these possibilities remain just that: possibilities (and an argument from silence) because we have no such coins in identifiably Alpine find spots. But whoever eventually finds any such datable Punic numismatic artifacts in the Alps – assuming that will happen – will have to work through these and possibly other permutations in order to quantify such chronologic events.

Part of the dearth of Carthaginian coins in circulation after the end of the Second Punic War circa 202 is due to assimilation into Roman coinage, but this may ultimately prove lucky in alpine finds that would be more likely to then represent Hannibal or Hasdrubal's passages: "Analysis of hoards across Italy, Sicily and Spain shows that all Carthaginian coinage in these areas was swept away after Rome's victory. It was melted down for recycling and replaced by Roman coins." [130] Thus any alpine coin finds as

126

described from Hannibal or Hasdrubal would be among the most likely archaeological evidence of the Carthaginians' routes than random survival. When I recently inquired of numismatist and fellow archaeologist Paolo Visona about the possibilities of distinguishing separate Hannibal/Hasdrubal coin issues, here is Visona's reply:

*"At least two of Hannibal's Italian issues come to mind which, in my view, are linked to Barcid issues in various ways. So, at least in theory, it should be feasible to pursue this project."*

## Conclusions

Thus, decisive Punic-issued numismatic evidence from Hannibal's alpine campaign could be part of the clinching chronometric material (optimum if along with other artifactual evidence such as human or elephant and other pack animal bones and radiocarbon dated wood or charcoal remains, etc.) to resolve part of this difficult historic question if the circumstances were as described above in just the right combination of factors.

## Chapter Eleven

## HANNIBAL BARCA'S THEOPHORIC DESTINY

### Introduction

That Hannibal was a great strategist, unpredictable himself yet often able to predict his enemies' actions, has been long appreciated. This is usually all one needs to know as an answer to why Hannibal crossed the Alps. Because the Romans under Publius Cornelius Scipio at Massalia guarded the coastal route to Italy hemmed in by the Alpes Maritimes, Hannibal did the one thing for which the Romans were most unprepared, not being fond of mountains themselves as Hyde maintained,[131] and thinking themselves protected from such unlikely incursions such as Hannibal and his army made, entering Italy through the "fortress" Alps. Naturally, the Celts allied to Hannibal in and around the Alps would also be more useful if he avoided the narrow coastal corridor where Roman might and influence held sway.

But are these the only background reasons to consider when asking why Hannibal would cross the Alps? I would argue that Hannibal was predisposed to crossing the Alps for added possible philosophical reasons the practical Romans would have barely understood, hence their likely silence on this because their own names were not generally theophoric, and usually unrelated to their gods, unlike the Carthaginians and many other cultures in the Ancient Near East.

Here it is important to consider Hannibal's very name and personal history to be important as a subtler but nonetheless substantial incentive or at least mitigating factor for crossing the Alps. There are also connections to Punic religious tradition that make more sense in reference to this possibility.

## Punic Tradition and Hannibal's youth

If the momentous account of Hannibal's joining his father Hamilcar Barca is to be trusted, it is important to also consider Phoenician and Punic archaeology from Carthage. According to Polybius (*Hist.* 3.11.5-8), Hamilcar would only bring his son with him to Spain if the nine-year-old boy would swear eternal enmity against Rome at the Carthage altar, most likely of Ba'al and possibly of Tanit, Ba'al's female consort, important Punic deities. Polybius specifically says the vow was made not only at the altar but that Hamilcar his father made him lay his hand on the sacrificial victim while making his oath.

For Roman readers, this graphic idea of a physically highlighted oath at a Punic altar may have been intended to evoke horrific ideas, but regardless of what Punic traditions the Romans understood (or misunderstood), if the event was historical, this needs contextualization with what we know about Punic child sacrifice. The *tophet* of Carthage, the precinct of Tanit who was the female consort of Ba'al, evidences a long tradition that would be familiar to Hamilcar and Hannibal even if not a normative practice. Ba'al ritual could require male child sacrifice if we accept Diodorus Siculus (*Library of History* XIII.86, XX.14), Silius Italicus (*Punica* IV.765-822), and Plutarch (*De superstitione* 171 C-D) - admittedly all Roman and possibly biased- in context with the excavations of Lawrence Stager and others at Carthage. [132] Although the debate still rages about this Punic ritual as either sensationalized on the one hand into normative human sacrifice or sanitized on the other hand into temporary crisis-related ritual killing,[133] thousands of excavated urns containing carbonized infant remains may ultimately prove Diodorus and others were not merely inventing Roman propaganda against Carthage. The impact of such Punic sacrifices or ritual tradition on a nine-year-old boy, possibly knowing of others slightly younger (perhaps even siblings or relatives) who could have been "sacrificed" or somehow made sanctified to Ba'al in death, might have been enormous on Hannibal's young life. If vows to Ba'al ever required live sacrifice of males, where older Ugaritic stelae (Figure 51) and inscriptions are applicable, the putative historical event gains importance. If young Hannibal could go to the altar of Ba'al and walk away as a votary, this ought to have been a very formative life experience as Polybius suggests.

**51. BA'AL RELIEF STELE – LATE BRONZE AGE**

*Linguistic and theophoric connections*

When this votive possibility is connected to his name, both personal and to his familial clan, his individual destiny seems more understandable. Much of the ancient world (with the seeming exception of Rome) commonly used theophoric names – personal names that contained their divinities – in such a way as to create a special relationship with a god or to forge individual destiny, whether subliminal as we might now understand such motivation or by conscious modeling to live up to a name as intended. This is where Hannibal's name would be especially important: Hannibal in Punic-Phoenician (*HANNI-BA'AL – HNB'L*) means "Ba'al be gracious to me" [134] or "Ba'al show favor to me" [135] and can probably be extended to related theophoric ideas from the noun-participle names compounded to express the relationship of the name-bearer to the divinity. [136] Hannibal's name is not uncommon for Phoenician-Punic cultures [137] but this does not diminish but rather enhances his association with such an important Punic deity.

Did this theophoric name also factor into the boy's being either spared by Ba'al or allowed to make a votive to the god, young as he was? This theophoric name would have been important to its bearer in ways later secular cultures can hardly begin to imagine, especially if Carthaginian religious devotion can in any way be measured by the *tophet* with its many excavated infant burial urns are to be taken seriously (some suggest a total estimate around at least 20,000 such "ritual burials" roughly between the 7th-2nd centuries BCE). It is difficult for a modern era to comprehend how much the supernatural dominated the mindset and behavioral praxis in antiquity. Hannibal's putative vow at the altar of Ba'al underscores the gravity of such religious fidelity. But the name of Hannibal's Barcid clan offers more: "Barca" from *brq* in Punic-Phoenician means "lightning" [138] as well as extrapolated from its earlier Ugaritic sources. [139] This phenomenon of lightning is also under the domain of Ba'al, a storm god who throws thunderbolts, as so many Ugaritic and Phoenician texts and archaeological artifacts such as Ba'al relief sculpture and statuettes with arms possibly holding the bolt suggest.[140] As one of the primary purveyors of fertility in successive Canaanite, Phoenician and Punic cultures, Ba'al is shown by association with sacred mountains and sacred stone. [141] Thus, Hannibal was doubly associated with Ba'al by his full name. If his vow against the Romans was also to Ba'al, the potential in the theophoric connection is further strengthened.


*Conclusions*


The ultimate implication, however, takes these theophoric name connections even further. Ba'al's primary domain is not just that of a storm god: he is also the god of holy mountains where such storms are born that fertilize the land. Mt. Saphon or (Saphan - Zaphon) in Syria (now known as Jebel Akra) was the landmark for north at Ugarit as well as Ba'al's holy mountain, often crowned with rain-laden clouds in the Ugaritic texts as well as in fact.[142]   Mt. Hermon in the interior and Mt. Lebanon (Libanus) above the coast were its southern counterparts for Phoenician peoples, but in fact all such mountains would have been Ba'al's domain regardless of landscape, [143] including around Jebel Chemtou (Simittou) and the Atlas Mountains to the southwest of Carthage.[144] The question is whether Hannibal might have been far more predisposed to challenge the Alps since his personal god was a god of mountains (Figure 52), a god whose domain was the very sacred locus of storms as well as rain and snow. From Hannibal's youth onward, his very name with all its theophoric connotations, "Ba'al's favored" and a member of the "lightning" Barcid clan, may have

**52. HANNIBAL'S ALPS?**

influenced his decision to enter and pass through a formidable range of mountains where others might not have dared. Even the Romans whose Jovian storm god was a western parallel may not have made this connection with Hannibal's theophoric name as the later Flavian temple of Jupiter Poeninus in the Alps was one where travelers hardly loitered. [145]

Did Hannibal also see it as his destiny to endure the heights and stormy hardships of the Alps, making him more able to cross with an army because he was under the protection of his personal mountain storm god Ba'al whose name and favor he bore? The immediate prospects for archaeological research on Hannibal by the Stanford Alpine Archaeology Project has been greatly enhanced by our sponsorship from the National Geographic Society and a 2007-2008 major grant from their Expedition Council for the upcoming Hannibal Expeditions.

# NOTES

*Chapter One*

[1]  Andrew S. Goudie, ed. *Encyclopedia of Global Change*, vols. 1-2. Oxford University Press, 2002, 112.

[2]  Ludwig Pauli. *The Alps: Archaeology and Early History*. London: Thames and Hudson, 1984.

[3]  In archaeology, there is a transitional period now accepted between Neolithic and Bronze Ages, certainly visible in the Alps.  See P. T. Craddock. *Early Metal Mining and Production*. Edinburgh University Press, 1995;  A. B. Knapp, V. C.  Pigott and E. W. Herbert, eds. *Social Approaches to an Industrial Past: The Archaeology and Anthropology of Mining*. London: Routledge, 1998; Stephen Shennan, "Producing copper in the eastern Alps during the second millennium BC" in  Knapp, Pigott and Herbert (eds), 1998, 191-204; R. Doonan, S. Klemm,  B. Ottaway, G. Sperl and H. Weinek. 'The East Alpine Bronze Age copper smelting process: evidence from the Ramsau Valley, Eisenerz, Austria." *Archaeometry 94 (1996)* 17-22;  Stephen Shennan. "Settlement and social change in central Europe, 3500-1500 BC." *Journal of World Prehistory* 7.2 (1993) 121-61.

[4]  C.B. Cox and Peter D. Moore. *Biogeography*. Oxford: Blackwell Scientific Publications, 1985, 4th ed.

[5]  T. M. Cronin. *Principles of Paleoclimatology*. New York: Columbia University Press, 1999.

[6]  H. E. Wright, J. E. Kutzbach, T. Webb, W. F. Ruddiman, F. A. Street-Perrott and P. J. Bartlein. *Global Climates Since the Last Glacial Maximum*. University of Minnesota Press, 1993, vital to understanding the last 18,000 years in Europe; R. C. L. Wilson, S. A. Drury and J. L. Chapman. *The Great Ice Age:  Climate Change and Life*. Routledge, 2000.

[7]  Peter Moore in David Attenborough, ed. *Atlas of the Living World*. Boston: Houghton Mifflin, 1989, 58.

[8]  *ibid.*

[9]  *loc. cit.*, 66.

[10]  *loc. cit.*, 72.

[11]  *loc. cit.*, 76

[12]  John Wallace, Peter Hobbs, *Atmospheric Science*, Volume 92, Second Edition: An Introductory Survey (International Geophysics), 2006; John Agnew, David Livingstone, Alisdair Rogers, eds. *Human Geography in Theory: An Essential Anthology*, Blackwells, 1996.

[13]  Moore in Attenborough, 1989, 78.

[14]  Marilyn Walker, Patrick Webber, Elizabeth Arnold and Diane Ebert-May. "Effects of interannual climate variation on aboveground phytomass in Alpine vegetation." *Ecology* 75.2 (1994) 393-408.

[15]  Goudie, 2002, 2:112-13.

[16]  Christoph Frei, Christian Haberli, Inga Groehn and Carlo Cacciamani. "Mesoscale Alpine Climate" in *MAP Newsletter* 14 (2001).

[17]  A. Blass, M. Grosjean and M. Sturm. "Quantitative high-resolution reconstruction of the Alpine climate since 1600 from varved Lake Silvaplana, eastern Swiss Alps: How stable are 20th century calibration models?" *Geophysical Research Abstracts* Vol. 8, o5872, European Geophysical Union (2006).

[18]  M. Laternser and M. Schneebeli. "Long-term snow climate trends of the Swiss Alps (1931-99)." *International Journal of Climatology* 23 (2003) 733-50.

[19]  Patrick Hunt. "Maya and Olmec Stone Contexts: Limestone and Basalt Weathering Contrasts." *Septima Mesa Redonda, Palenque 1989*, San Francisco: Precolumbian Art Research Institute, 1994, 261-67.

[20]  Brenda Fowler. *Iceman*. Pan, 2002.

*Chapter Two*

[21]  Note 2 above, Wright et al, 1993; Wilson et al, 2000.

[22]  Moore in Attenborough, 1989, 34.

[23]  M. Arnold. "The radiative effects of clouds and their impact on climate." *Bulletin of the American Meteorological Society* 72 (1991) 795-813.

[24] Philippe Della Casa. *Prehistoric alpine environment, society, and economy (PAESE, 1997). Papers of the International Kolloquium in Zurich. UPA 55.* Bonn: Habelt Verlag, 1999.

[25] Moore in Attenborough, 1989, 78.

[26] Henri de La Tour. *Atlas de Monnaies Gauloises,* 1878 ed.

[27] The Celtic Sequani coin was found in the Plan de Jupiter in Italy in a joint excavation sponsored by the Soprintendenza of the Val d'Aosta with the collaboration of the Stanford Alpine Archaeology Project in 2000.

[28] Konrad Spindler. *Derr Mann im Eis.* Ed. Betelsmann, 1993; M. Egg. "L'homme dans la glace." *Dossiers d'archeologie* Ed. Faton 224 (1997) 28-35; A. Bocquet. "Les Alpes occidentales francaises au temps de l'homme du Similaun, vers 3000 av. J.C." *Bulletin d'etudes prehistoriques et archéologiques alpines* VII-VIII (1996-97) 67-81.

[29] Johan Reinhard. *The Ice Maiden: Inca Mummies, Mountain Gods and Sacred Sites in the Andes.* National Geographic Society (reprint) 2006.

[30] Henrik Svensmark and Nigel Calder. *The Chilling Stars: A New Theory of Climate Change.* London: Icon Books, 2007 (paperback). Ch. 1.

[31] Donald Kennedy. *State of the Planet.* AAS-Science. Island Press, 2006, 47-8.

*Chapter Three*

[32] György Füleky, ed. *Soils and Archaeology.* First International Conference on Soils and Archaeology, Hungary 2001. BAR – Archaeopress S-1163, 2003; Vance T. Holliday. *Soils in Archaeological Research.* Oxford University Press, 2004.

[33] L. Nagy, G. Grabherr, C. Körner and D. B. Thompson. *Alpine Biodiversity in Europe.* Ecological Studies. Berlin: Springer Verlag, 2003.

[34] J. Jacob Parnell, Richard E. Terry, Payson Sheets. "Soil chemical analysis of ancient activities in Ceren, El Salvador: a case study of a rapidly abandoned site. (Reports)." *Latin American Antiquity,* Society for American Archaeology 2002.

[35] Timothy M. Wright. "Investigation of Soil pH at Cox's Woods Site, 12 Or" (1996)

http://www.gbl.indiana.edu/wright_doc.html. The findings in this report, while useful for demonstrating a range of microcontexts with different pH readings was nonetheless inconclusive for answering the question posed about bone survival.

[36]   Myra Shackley. *Environmental Archaeology*. London: Allen and Unwin, 1981, 46, 50.

[37]   Helen Smith, Peter Marshall and Mike Pearson, "Reconstructing house activity areas" in Umberto Albarella, ed. *Environmental Archaeology: Meaning and Purpose*. Dordrecht: Kluwers Academic Publishers, 2001, 252, 263.

[38]   Nick Branch, Matthew Canti, Peter Clark and Chris Turney. *Environmental Archaeology: Theoretical and Practical Approaches*. London: Hodder Arnold/Hodder Education, 2005, 50; S. J. Gale and P. G. Hoare. Quaternary Sediments: *Petrographic Methods for the Study of Unlithified Rocks*. London: Belhaven Press, 1991.

[39]   Linda Manzanilla and Luis Barba. "The Study of Activities in Classic Households. Two case studies from Coba and Teotihuacan." *Ancient Mesoamerica* 1, Cambridge University Press, 1990, 41-49; Linda Manzanilla. "Corporate groups and domestic activities at Teotihuacan", *Latin American Antiquity* 7.3 (1996) 228-246.

[40]   Donald Sparks. *Environmental Soil Chemistry*. San Diego: Academic Press, 1995, 203-16.

## Chapter Four

[41]   G. V. Dal Piaz. "The Austroalpine-Piedmont nappe stack and the puzzle of Alpine Tethys. " In G. Gosso et al., eds. *Third Meeting on Alpine Geol. Studies, Mem. Sci. Geol.*, 51 (1999) 155-176; E. M. Moores, R. W. Fairbridge, eds. *Encyclopedia of European and Asian Regional Geology* (Encyclopedia of Earth Sciences Series). Berlin: Springer Verlag, 1997.

[42]   S. Schmid, B. Fügenshuh, E. Kissling and R. Schuster. "Tectonic map and overall architecture of the Alpine orogen. *Eclogae Geologicae Helvetiae* 97 (2004); W. Frisch, I. Dunkl and J. Kuhlemann. "Post-collisional large-scale extension in the Eastern Alps." *Tectonophysics* 327 (2000).

[43]   D. R. Brothwell and A. M. Pollard, eds. *Handbook of Archaeological Sciences*. John Wiley, 2001. See "archaeological prospection".

[44]   George Rapp. *Archaeomineralogy*. Springer Verlag, 2002.

[45]   C. D'Amico. "Neolithic 'Greenstone' axe blades from Northwestern Italy across Europe: A first petrographic comparison" *Archaeometry* 47.2 (2005) 235-52.

[46]   John J. Hermann, Norman Herz and Richard Newman, eds. *Interdisciplinary Studies on Ancient Stone*. ASMOSIA 5. London: Archetype, 2002.

[47]   M. Unterwurzacher, J. Polleres, P. Mirwald, "Provenance study of marble artefacts from the Roman burial area of Faschendorf (Carinthia, Austria)" *Archaeometry* 47.2 (2005) 265-73.

[48]   Publications by this author on the Stanford Alpine Archaeology Project include: Patrick Hunt, "Summus Poeninus on the Grand St Bernard Pass", *Journal of Roman Archaeology* XI (1998) 265-74; Patrick Hunt, "Plan de Barasson: Refuge romain et aqueduc" ["Plan de Barasson: Roman refuge and aqueduct"] in F. Wiblé, ed. *Vallesia: Chronique des découvertes archéologiques dans le canton du Valais in 1998,* tr. M. Pignolet. LXIV (1999) 300-8; Patrick Hunt, "Romans in the Alps: Summus Poeninus" in *AIA Abstracts, vol. 24, 102nd Annual Meeting* (2000) 51; Patrick Hunt, "Bronze Tabulae Ansatae at Roman Summus Poeninus in the Roman Alps" *in Acta: From the Parts to the Whole*, volume 2 of the XIIIth International Bronze Congress, Harvard University Art Museum, *JRA* Supplement (2002) .

[49] Grand-St-Bernard. Feuille 33 de l'Atlas de Suisse (corresponding to CNS 1365). *Atlas Geologique de la Suisse*. Explanatory notes by N. Oulianoff and R. Trumpy. Bern: Commission Geologique Suisse, 1958, esp. note p. 37 on the calc-schists of the Fenetre de Ferret.  Also see *Tabula Imperii Romani*  (TIR) Mediolanum Plate 1966

[50]   Mark. Meier. "Glaciers" in M. McCracken and John Perry, eds. *Encyclopedia of Global Environmental Change*, vol. 1. New York: John Wiley, 2002, 404-05 & ff..

[51] Roger Mason. *Petrology of the Metamorphic Rocks*. London: George Allen & Unwin, 1978, 33; B.W.D. Yardley, W.S. MacKenzie and C. Guilford. *Atlas of Metamorphic Rocks and Their Textures*. 1990 ed., 15-7, 57-8.

[52] P. N. Hunt and D.R. Griffiths. "Optical Petrology in the Field" in *World Archaeology* 21.1 (1989) 165-72.

[53] Patrick Hunt. "Inca Volcanic Stone Provenance in the Cuzco Province, Peru", *Papers of the Institute of Archaeology* Vol. 1, 1990, 24-36; Patrick Hunt. *Provenance, Weathering and Technology of Selected Basalts and Andesites*. Ph.D. Dissertation, Institute of Archaeology, UCL, University of London, 1991; Patrick Hunt. "Olmec Stone Sculpture: Criteria of Stone Selection" in *Volcanoes, Earthquakes and Archaeology*, London: Royal Geological Society of London, 2000, 345-53. Acknowledgements are due to Yvonne Bergero for discovery of the old original 11th c. monastery door and to Gary Bergero for reconstructing a CGI 3-D Temple model in color.

## Chapter Five

[54] A. Planta, "Zum romischen Weg uber den Grossen St. Bernhard" *Helvetia Archaeologica* 37, 1979, esp. 20-28.

[55] Hunt *JRA* XI (1998), esp. 266-69 & n12-13; P. Hunt in F. Wible, ed. "A Roman Refuge in Plan de Barasson" in *Vallesia* LIV (1999) 303-8.

[56] *Spolium* as "arms or armour stripped from a defeated enemy" Livy 1, 10, 6 (*spolia ducis hostium...regia arma fero templumque dedico*). Spolia or Spoils of War as a Classical tradition can be seen in early on in *Spolia opima* dedicated in the temple of Jupiter Feretrius by a victorious Roman general who had slain an equal enemy in combat. cf. Piero Treves, *Oxford Classical Dictionary* on *spolia opima*, 1949, 857; Dale Kinney. "Roman Architectural Spolia" in *Proceedings of the American Philosophical Society* 145.2 (2001) 138-150 plus figures.

[57] Tim Eaton. "Old ruins, new world" in *British Archaeology* vol. 60. August, 2001.

[58] L. Blondel, "L'Eglise et le Prieure de Bourg-St-Pierre." *Vallesia* I, Sion, 1946, pp. 21-41; *Archives of Castellum Sancti Petri*: 2.500 Anni. Bourg-St-Pierre.

[59] Msgr. Marius Besson, *Nos origines chretiennes*, Fribourg, 1921; L. Quaglia, *La Maison du Grand-St-Bernard,* Imprimerie Pillet, Martigny, 1972, XIX-XXI. This monastery was attached to the Diocese of Sion and nominally connected to the Diocese of Lausanne.

[60] R. Latouche, "Les idees actuelles sur les Sarrasins dan les Alpes" in *Revue de geographie alpine.*" Tome XIX, Grenoble, 1931, 199-206.

[61] Hunt *JRA* XI 265.

[62] *ibid.* 269

[63] G. Walser, "Summus Poeninus", *Historia*, Heft 46, Zurich, 1984, Plates 16 & ff.

[64] This epigraphic reading of *VESP[ASIANUS]* was first suggested in 1996 by Francois Wible, Cantonal Archaeologist of the Valais and independently suggested in summer 1996 by the Stanford Alpine Archaeological team, specifically by Irene Polinskaya. This new reading supersedes prior readings of, for example, *VFS[__]* and others (cf. Blondel in 1946, Walser in 1984, etc.). Both Francois Wible in 1997 and Patrick Hunt in 1998 have subsequently published this reading in separate venues in Europe and elsewhere.

[65] Pontifex Maximus: G. Wissowa, *Religion und Kultus der Romer*, 1912; H.J. Rose, *Oxford Classical Dictionary*, 1949, 716; L. Adkins and R. A. Adkins, *Dictionary of Roman Religion*, 1996, 182.

[66] F. Wiblé, "Le temple de Jupiter Poeninus, au sommet du Col du Grand-St-Bernard, erige ou reconstruit a l'epoque flavienne?" *Bulletin d'Etudes prehistoriques alpines*, VII-VIII, 1996-97, 19-26; Hunt, *JRA* XI 266.

*Chapter Six*

[67] L. Blondel. "La route romaine du Mont Joux" in *Hommage à A. Genier*, Brussells, (1962) I, 308-15.

[68] G. Walser. *Summus Poeninus. Historia*, Heft 46 (1984).

[69] F. Wiblé, ed. "Cols et communications: La route du col du Gd St-Bernard." *Vallis Poenina: La Valais à l'époque romaine*. Sion: Musée cantonal d'archéologie (1999); also "Le traffic commercial par le Grand Saint Bernard a la époque romaine: l'apport de l'épigraphie et de quelques données archéologiques" in *Alpis Graia: Archeologie sans frontiers au col de Petit-Saint-Bernard*. Italia-Franchia ALCOTRA Projet Interreg IIIA (2006) 285-89.

[70] A. Planta. "Zum römischen Weg über den Grossen St Bernhard" *Archaeologica Helvetia* 37 (1979) 15-30.

[71] R. Mollo Mazzena. *Viae publicae romana*. Aosta (1991) 235-42.

[72] W. W. Hyde. *Roman Alpine Routes*. Philadelphia: American Philosophical Society, 1935.

[73] See *Bibliography* here for this book.

[74] L. Casson. "Roman Roads", ch. 10. *Travel in the Ancient World*. Allen and Unwin (1974) 163-75 (reprinted by Johns Hopkins, 1994 ed.).

[75] R. Chevallier. *Roman Roads*. Berkeley: University of California, (1976), translation, applicable here esp. in 85-92.

[76] L. A. and J. A. Hamey. *The Roman Engineers*. Cambridge University Press (1981).

[77] K. D. White. *Greek and Roman Technology*, London: Thames and Hudson (1989).

*Chapter Seven*

[78] François Wiblé. "Quelques reflexions sur la 'romanisation' du Mont Joux, in Ceux qui passent et cuex qui restent, Études sur le traffics transalpins et leur impact local." *Actes du Colloque de Bourg-Saint-Pierre 1988* (1989) 191-204.

[79] Lucan gave too much prominence to familiar Celtic deity names (e.g., Teutates, Esus in Pharsalia I.444-6 *et quibus inmitis placatur sanguine diro Teutates horrensque feris altaribus Esus et Taranis Scythicae non mitior ara Dianae.*) without being able to verify how or where they stood within the Celtic pantheon of deities or whether they might be merely epithets of tribal gods. Caesar also often reduced Celtic deities to particular recognizable Roman correspondences like Mars; cf. T. G. E. Powell. The Celts. London: Thames and Hudson,1995 repr., 158 & ff.

[80] François Wiblé. "Considérations sur la romanisation des vallées latérales en Valais." *Bulletin d'Études préhistoriques alpines*, 15 (1983) 189-93.

[81] W. W. Hyde. *Roman Alpine Routes*. Mem. Am. Phil. Soc. Vol. II (Philadelphia,1935),61, 107 n 122. The *roche sacré* was part of the Celtic shrine in a tradition of *solis columna*, also with Raetian connections to the Julier pass and the Ceutrones at the Little St. Bernard pass.

[82] Polybius 3. 34.10

[83]   P. Hunt, *JRA* XI (1998) 266 & ff;  P. Hunt. "Plan de Barasson: Refuge romain et aqueduc" (1999) 302 ff.

[84]   Julius Caesar, *De Bello Gallico* III.1; Polybius XXXIV.10; Strabo 4.6.12; Pliny, *Hist. Nat.* III.123 (*Alpes Graiae et Poeninae*);  Tacitus, *Historiae* I.61.1 and I.70.3 (*monts Poenins, Poenins*), among others.

[85]   Patrick Hunt. "Alpine Archaeology: Stone Sourcing of a Jupiter Temple and Petrographic Provenance." *Archaeolog (Stanford) 2006.* http://traumwerk.stanford.edu/archaeolog/2006/01/sourcing_stone_provenancing_p e.html

[86]   François Wiblé et al. *Vallis Poenina: La Valais à l'époque romaine.* Sion: Musée cantonal d'archéologie, 1998, 111, 165-75.

[87]   *ibid.,* 102-3.

[88]   Maxence Segard. "Les sociétés alpines à l'époque romaine au travers des types d'habitat et des modes de construction" in *Alpis Graia: Archeologie sans frontiers au col de Petit-Saint-Bernard.* Italia-Franchia ALCOTRA Projet Interreg IIIA (2006) 337-40,  esp. fig. 2.

[89]   Olivier Paccolat. "Le village gallo-romain de Brigue-Glis/Waldmatte. Archéologie Suisse 20.1 (1997) 25-36.

[90]   Henri de la Tour. *Atlas de Monnaies Gauloises.* Paris: Editions Plon 1968.

[91]   Kristian Kristiansen. *Europe before History.* Cambridge: Cambridge University Press, 1998, 415 & ff.

[92]   A. Zanco. "Provenance and technology of Gallo-Roman Terra Sigillata imitations from Western Switzerland." *Plinius* 21 (1999) 139-143.

[93]   Seppi:  Rooftile *Fabricator,* 1st c. CE in Val d'Aosta;  s.v.  C.  Promis, *Le antichita di Aosta.* Mem Accad. Scienze, ser. II. Vol. 2 Torino, 1864;  P. Barocelli, *Inscript, Ital.* XI.1 [Augusta Praetoria] Rome, 1932;  R. Mollo Mazzena, *Viae publicae romana,* Aosta, 1991, 235-42.

[94]   Some ceramic descriptions are from publications of Roman ceramics such as: C. Orton, *Pottery Archive Users handbook.* Museum of London, rev. 1984; K. Greene, *Roman Pottery,* London, British Museum, 1992, esp. 10-16.

[95] A. A. V. V. "Ceramique romaine en Suisse." *Antiqua* 31 Basel. 1999.

[96] Donald Bailey. *Catalogs of the lamps in the British Museum*. 3-4: Roman Provincial lamps and stone and metal lamps. London: British Museum, 1988 & 1996; Laurent Chrzanovski. *Lumieres Antiques: les lampes à huile*. Nyon: Musee Romain Nyon, 2000.

[97] D. Paunier. *La céramique gallo-romain de Genève*. Musee d'Art et d' Histoire, Geneve, 1981; Groupe de travail sure les Sigillées claire, Céramiques tardives à revetement argileux des Alpes du nord e de la vallée du Rhone [de Martigny à Vienne] *Figlina* 7 (1986) 19-49.

[98] Cinzia Joris. "I Materiali di Scavo Provenienti dall'Edificio sud del Plan de Jupiter: Considerazioni Preliminari" in *Alpis Graia: Archeologie sans frontiers au col de Petit-Saint-Bernard*. Italia-Franchia ALCOTRA Projet Interreg IIIA (2006) 305-14.

[99] T. Mommsen. *Inscriptiones Confoederationis Helveticae Latinae*. (Zurich, 1854) as *CIL* V 6863-6894; E. Ferrero and P. Castelfranco. *Scavi nell'area del tempio Giove Penino, Gran San Bernardo* (Torino, 1890-1894); P. Barocelli. "Ricerche e studi sui monumenti romani della Val d'Aosta." *Rivista della Provincia*, Anno VI (1934)72; G. Walser. *Summus Poeninus, Beiträge zur Geschichte des Grossen St. Bernhard-Passes in römischer Zeit* (*Historia Einzelschriften* 46) Wiesbaden, 1984; P. Hunt. "Bronze Tabulae Ansatae at Roman Summus Poeninus in the Roman Alps" *Acta: From the Parts to the Whole*, vol. 2, *Proceedings of XIIIth International Bronze Congress*, Harvard University Art Museums, JRA Supplement (2002).

[100] P. Hunt, *JRA* XI (1998) 270-1.

[101] Patrick Hunt. "Alpine Archaeology: Some Effects of Altitude and Climate." *Archaeolog* (Stanford) 2005 http://traumwerk.stanford.edu/archaeolog/2005/12/some_effects_of_altitude_and_c.html

[102] Kristiansen, 63-4 and especially 120.

## Chapter Eight

[103]   F. W. Walbank. " Some Reflections on Hannibal's Pass." *Journal of Roman Studies* (1956) 37-45.

[104]   Polybius. *History*, Book III, Chapters 53-60. Also 34.10.

[105]   C. Torr. *Hannibal Crosses the Alps*. Cambridge: Cambridge University Press, 1925.

[106]   M. A. de Lavis-Trafford. *Le col alpin franchi par Hannibal*. Saint-Jean-de-Maurienne, 1956.

[107]   Sir Gavin de Beer. *Alps and Elephants*. London: Bles, 1955; *Hannibal: The Struggle for Power in the Mediterranean*. London: Thames and Hudson, 1969.

[108]   Walbank. 37-45.

[109]   Eduard Meyer. "Hannibals Alpenubergang" in *Museum Helveticum* 15, 1953, 227-241.

[110]   Ernle Bradford. *Hannibal*. London: Macmillan, 1981.

[111]   Serge Lancel, *Hannibal*, Blackwells, 1999.

## Chapter Nine

[112]   John Hoyte. *Alpine Elephant: In the Tracks of Hannibal*, Fabrizio, (1960) 1975 ed.

[113]   John Prevas. *Hannibal Crosses the Alps: The Invasion of Italy and the Second Punic War*. Perseus/Da Capo, 1998.

[114] Christian Schlüchter and Ueli Jörin. "Alpen ohne Gletscher? : Holz- und Torffundeals Klimaindikatoren" *Die Alpe*, June, 2004, 35-46.

[115] Spenser Wilkinson. *Hannibal's March through the Alps*. Oxford: Clarendon Press, 1911; Douglas Freshfield. "Hannibal Once More" : review of *Hannibal's March through the Alps*." *The Geographical Journal* 37.4 (1911) 398-407;  R. L. Dunbabin. "Notes on Livy. I." *The Classical Review* 45.2 (1931) 52-57.

[116]   Adrian Goldsworthy. *The Punic Wars*. London: Cassell & Co, 2000, 163-66.

[117] John Hazel. "Hannibal" in *Who's Who in the Roman World*. London: Routledge, 2006 repr. , 132.

[118] Serge Lancel, *Hannibal*, 1999 (see above). Lancel follows Lavis-Traffort and Meyer to favor the Savine-Coche exit at the very terminus of the Clapier route on the southern path (only a kilometer from the regular Clapier path's descent). I have followed both these paths to where they merge again a little way below the main summit on the Italian side of the descent.

[119] Geoffroy de Galbert. *Hannibal en Gaule*. Belledonne, 2006.

[120] William C. Mahaney and Pierre Tricart. "The Unknown Gallic Commander: Hannibal';s Debacle in the Combe de Queyras in 218 BC." Nottingham, Military Geography Conference, 2005; also same conference, W. C. Mahaney, Volli Kolm and Randy Dirszowsky. "The Hannibal invasion of Italia in 218 BC: Geological/topographical analysis of the invasion routes." In the latter, their opinion is "Correlation of geological / topographical variables of all possible approaches/cols in the Alps with the ancient literature reveals that the only gateway that could have been used is the southern [Traversette] route." I would like to see their study integrating more data collected and presented for Claper-Savine Coche, but I respect their conclusions.

## Chapter Ten

121 W. E. Metcalf. "Numismatics" in N. de Grummond, ed. *An Encyclopedia of the History of Classical Archaeology*, L-Z [vol 2.], Westport, CT: Greenwood Press (1996) 813-5.

122 Lorenza Ilia Manfredi. "Carthaginian Policy Through Coins" in Giovanna Pisano, ed. *Phoenicians and Carthaginians in the Western Mediterranean. Studia Punica* 12 (1999) 69-78.

123 Barry Cunliffe. *The Ancient Celts*. Oxford: Oxford University Press, 1997, 104.

124 Y. Meshorer. *Coins from the Ancient World*: Lerner Archaeology Series. Minneapolis: Lerner (1980) 47-50.

125 Jean-Baptiste Giard. "Review: Les Monnaies de Carthago Nova". *Journal of Roman Archaeology* VIII (1995) 359.

126 J. Cribb, Barry Cook, Ian Carradice. *The Coin Atlas*. New York: Facts on File, 1990, 51.

127 M. L. Uberti. *L'artigianato*: Z. Cherif. *Terres cuites puniques de Tunisie*. Rome (1997)

163-217, esp. 233; Enrico Acquaro. "The Shield of Hasdrubal." In Giovanna Pisano, ed. *Phoenicians and Carthaginians in the Western Mediterranean. Studia Punica* 12 (1999) 31-34, esp. 33.

[128]  P. Hunt, *JRA*, 1998:265, 270; P. Hunt, *Vallesia* LIV 1999, 300 ff and P. Hunt, *Archaeolog* (Stanford) April, 2006.

[129] Paolo Visona. "Punic and Greek Bronze Coins from Carthage." *American Journal of Archaeology (AJA)* 89.4 (1985) 671-5, esp. 674-5 & Table B.

[130] Simon Denison. "Coins Reveal How Hannibal Bankrupted the Romans". *British Archaeology* 71 (July, 2003).

*Chapter Eleven*

[131]  W. W. Hyde. *Roman Alpine Routes*. Philadelphia: American Philosophical Society, 1935, i-iv & ff, 25-27.

[132]  Henry Hurst, Lawrence E. Stager. "A Metropolitan Landscape: The Late Punic Port of Carthage" *World Archaeology* 9.3 (1978) 334-346; Joseph Greene. *Punic Project Excavations: Child Sacrifice in the Context of Carthaginian Religion: Excavations in the Tophet*, American Schools of Oriental Research; Lawrence E. Stager and Samuel R. Wolff, "Child Sacrifice at Carthage: Religious Rite or Population Control? *Biblical Archaeology Review*, January/February 1984.

[133]  Brien Garnand. "From Infant sacrifice to the ABC's: Ancient Phoenicians and Modern Identities." *Narrative Pasts / Past Narratives Conference*, Stanford, 2001.

[134] Charles R. Krahmalkov. *Phoenician-Punic Dictionary. Studia Phoenicia* XV Orientalia Lovaniensia Analecta 90. Leuven: Peeters, 2000, 190.

[135] From *HNN* "to be kind, show favor" in Ugaritic. Richard S. Tomback. *A Comparative Semitic Lexicon of the Phoenician and Punic Languages*. Society of Biblical Literature Dissertation Series 32. Missoula: Scholars Press, 1978, 109.

[136] Zellig S. Harris. *A Grammar of the Phoenician Language*. New Haven: American Oriental Society, 1936, 66 but also 61, 103.

[137] Krahmalkov, 190.

[138] Frank Benz. *Personal Names in the Phoenician and Punic Inscriptions*. Studia Pohl. Rome: Biblical Institute Press, 1972, 292.

[139] Cyrus Gordon. *Ugaritic Textbook*: Grammar, Texts, Glossary, Indices. Analecta Orientalia 38. Rome: Pontificium Institutum Biblicum,1965, 377 (brq = Glossary Entry 524).

[140] For a good example, see the Ba'al stele relief sculpture, circa 18th-15th c. BCE from the Louvre, AO 15775 as Fig. 1 here shows; also see Y. Yadin. *Hazor*, Schweich Lectures on Biblical Archaeology. Oxford: Oxford University Press, 1972, 101 & ff.; Claude Schaeffer. *Ugaritica* IV. Ras Shamra Excavations. Paris: Imprimerie Nationale, 1962. The figure used here of a horned Ba'al has been variously interpreted as holding a thunderbolt or a mace, and the decorative undulation at the stela base has also been interpreted as mountains and/or a river.

[141] Patrick Hunt. "Canaanite Use of Basalt and Related Provenance Research" Chapter 7, *Provenance, Weathering and Technology of Selected Archaeological Basalts and Andesites*. Ph.D. Dissertation, Institute of Archaeology, UCL, University of London, 1991, 199-252, esp. 206-8 regarding Hazor.

[142] P. N. Hunt. "Mt. Saphon in Myth and Fact" in E. Lipinski, ed. *Studia Phoenicia* XI. *Phoenicia and the Bible*. Orientalia Lovaniensia Analecta 44. Leuven: Peeters, 1991, 103-15; H. Ginserg in J.B. Pritchard, ed. *Ancient Near Eastern Texts (A.N.E.T.)*, Vol. 1, Princeton, 1958, 101,103, 108.

[143] Gabriele Borghini, ed. *Marmi antichi*. Rome: Ministero per i Beni Culturali e Ambientale/ Edizioni de Luca, 1997, 214-15 pl.65; A. Bowman, A. Cameron and P. Garnsey, eds. *The Cambridge Ancient History*, vol 12, (2005) 2nd. ed., 406. Although John Ward Perkins, specifically in "Tripolitania and the Marble Trade", *Journal of Roman Studies* 41 (1951) 88-105, shows the decorative colored marble (Giallo Numidiana) was used ostensibly for aesthetic criteria by Numidian kings prior to 78 BCE, (citing Pliny, *Nat. Hist*, XXXVI.49 *marmor Numidicum*) which Amanda Claridge, *Rome: Oxford Archaeological Guides* (1998) 40 also notes, the stone from this specifc mountain range (now Jebel Chemtou) was already sacralized by Punic culture through Ba'al association with these mountains, a metaphysical criterion established by this author elsewhere

(e.g. first in chapter 2 of the Ph.D. dissertation, 1991, already cited in note 11 above).

[144] C. F. A. Schaeffer. *The Cuneiform Texts of Ras-Shamra-Ugarit*. London: British Academy, Schweich Lectures. 1939, 70-1; J. Gray. *The Legacy of Canaan* (Supplements to *Vetus Testamentum* 5). Leiden: E. J. Brill, 1965, 148. For Ba'al as a general mountain storm god, see H. Ginsberg in *A.N.E.T., op. cit.*, 102, lines 70 & ff.

[145] Hunt (1998) esp. 265-69

# PHOTO CREDITS

1  "ALPINE SCHRECKHORN" courtesy  www.caingram.info/Europe web
2  "ALPINE MAP" Public Domain Web
3  "ALPINE VEGETATION ZONES" courtesy Swiss National Atlas
4  "ALPINE CLIMATE" courtesy Swiss National Atlas
5  "ALPINE CLIMATE - TEMPERATURE MAP" courtesy Swiss National Atlas
6  "ALPINE CLIMATE -  OTZI ICEMAN" Public Domain Free News Web
7  "pH ALPINE JUNIPER" Moosfluh, Valais, courtesy Villardebelle Arboretum, France.
8  "pH ALPINE AZALEA" courtesy University of Florida (MG092)
9  "pH  SCALE" Public Domain Web
10  "ALPINE GEOMORPHOLOGY" courtesy Swiss National Atlas
11  "ALPINE JUPITER TEMPLE" G. Bergero
12  "JUPITER TEMPLE STONE IN MONASTERY FLOOR" P. Hunt
13  "JUPITER TEMPLE STONE IN MONASTERY VAULT" P. Hunt
14  "ALPINE FIELD GEOLOGY" P. Hunt
15  "ALPINE GEOLOGY PROVENANCE" C.H.I.
16  "ALPINE SPOLIA BOURG-ST-PIERRE" Public Domain Web
17  "ALPINE SPOLIA MILESTONE" E. Pirrotta
18  "ALPINE SPOLIA EPIGRAPHY" E. Pirrotta
19  "ALPINE ROMAN ROADS MAP" courtesy Tabula Romani Imperii
20  "ALPINE ROAD STANFORD ARCHAEOLOGY TEAM 1994" P. Hunt
21  "ALPINE ROCK CUT ROAD ANGLE" P. Hunt
22  "ALPINE GSB ROAD DESCENT" B. Foster
23  "ALPINE ROAD EXCAVATION X-SECTION" P. Hunt
24  "ALPINE ROUTE GSB PASS" courtesy GoogleEarth / P. Hunt
25  "ALPINE ROAD EXCAVATION – P. HUNT" P. Hunt
26  "ALPINE GALLO-ROMAN TEMPLE, MARTIGNY" courtesy F. Wiblé, O.R.A.
27  "ALPINE GALLO-ROMAN 'BARN' " P. Hunt
28  "ALPINE COINS ROMAN & GAULISH" C.H.I. (Cultural Heritage Imaging)
29  "STAMPED ROMAN TEGULAE" C.H.I.
30  "STAMPED TEGULAE DISTRIBUTION" C.H.I.
31  "ROMAN CERAMICS" C.H.I.
32  "GALLO-ROMAN CERAMICS" C.H.I.
33  "TABULA ANSATA" C.H.I.
34  "PLAN DE BARASSON STRATIGRAPHY" C.H.I.
35  "HANNIBAL IN THE ALPS" Public Domain Web
36  "SAVINE DENTS D'AMBIN" Joel Ble
37  "BRAMANS 'BARE ROCK'  PLACE" E. Pirrotta / Marlin Lum
38  "CLAPIER-SAVINE CATTLE" M. Lum / C.H.I.

# BIBLIOGRAPHY

E. Acquaro, L. I. Manfredi and A. Cutroni Tusa. *Le monete puniche in Italia*, Roma (1991).

John Agnew, David Livingstone, Alisdair Rogers, eds. *Human Geography in Theory: An Essential Anthology*, Blackwells, 1996.

David Attenborough, ed. *Atlas of the Living World*. Boston: Houghton Mifflin, 1989.

L. Blondel. "La route romaine du Mont Joux" in *Hommage à A. Genier*, Brussells, (1962) I, 308-15.

Ernle Bradford. *Hannibal*. London: Macmillan, 1981, 60 ff.

L. Casson. "Roman Roads", ch. 10. *Travel in the Ancient World*. Allen and Unwin (1974) 163-75 (now reprinted by Johns Hopkins).

R. Chevallier. *Roman Roads*. Berkeley: University of California, (1976), translation, applicable here esp. in 85-92.

C.B. Cox and Peter D. Moore. *Biogeography*. Oxford: Blackwell Scientific Publications, 1985, 4th ed.

T. M. Cronin. *Principles of Paleoclimatology*. New York: Columbia University Press, 1999.

Barry Cunliffe. *The Ancient Celts*. Oxford: Oxford University Press, 1997.

A. Cutroni Tusa. "La politica monetaria di Cartagine." *Considerazioni: studi in onore di S. Moscati* Roma (1996) 111-5.

Philippe Della Casa. *Prehistoric alpine environment, society, and economy (PAESE, 1997). Papers of the International Kolloquium in Zurich. UPA* 55. Bonn: Habelt Verlag, 1999.

R. L. Dunbabin. "Notes on Livy. I." *The Classical Review* 45.2 (1931) 52-57.

M. Egg. "L'homme dans la glace." *Dossiers d'archeologie* Ed. Faton 224 (1997) 28-35.

Brenda Fowler. *Iceman*. Pan, 2002.

Douglas Freshfield. "Hannibal Once More" : review of *Hannibal's March through the Alps." The Geographical Journal* 37.4 (1911) 398-407.

György Füleky, ed. *Soils and Archaeology*. First International Conference on Soils and Archaeology, Hungary 2001. BAR – Archaeopress S-1163, 2003.

Geoffroy de Galbert. *Hannibal en Gaule*. Belledonne, 2006.

L. A. and J. A. Hamey. *The Roman Engineers*. Cambridge University Press (1981).

Vance T. Holliday. *Soils in Archaeological Research*. Oxford University Press, 2004.

John Hoyte. *Alpine Elephant: In the Tracks of Hannibal*. Palo Alto: Fabrizio, 1975 repr.

J. H. Humphries, ed. (T. V. Buttrey, "The Coins") *Excavations at Carthage 1975 Conducted by the University of Michigan* 1 (Tunis 1976) as well as subsequent publications through 1982 (Ann Arbor).

Patrick Hunt. "Summus Poeninus in the Grand St Bernard Pass". *Journal of Roman Archaeology* XI (1998) 264-74.

_____. "Plan de Barasson: Refuge romain et aqueduc" in F. Wible, ed. *VALLESIA: Chroniques des découvertes archéologiques dans le canton du Valais en 1998* LIV Sion (1999) 300-8.

_____. "Some Effects of Climate and Altitude on Alpine Archaeology". *Archaeolog* (Stanford University). Nov. 2005.

_____. "Alpine Archaeology: Hannibal in the Alps." *Archaeolog*, (Stanford University),April, 2006.
(http://traumwerk.stanford.edu/archaeolog/2006/04/hannibal_in_the_alps_stanford_ 1.html)

G. Kenneth Jenkins and R. B. Lewis. *Carthaginian Gold and Electrum Coins*, London: Royal Numismatics Society (1963).

Cinzia Joris. "I Materiali di Scavo Provenienti dall'Edificio sud del Plan de Jupiter: Considerazioni Preliminari" in *Alpis Graia: Archeologie sans frontiers au col de Petit-Saint-Bernard*. Italia-Franchia ALCOTRA Projet Interreg IIIA (2006) 305-14.

Serge Lancel. *Hannibal*. London: Blackwells, 1999.

R. Mollo Mazzena. *Viae publicae romana*. Aosta (1991) 235-42.

Theodore Mommsen. *Die Geschichte des römischen Munwesens*, Berlin (1861).

Ludwig Pauli. *The Alps: Archaeology and Early History*, (translated from German). London: Thames and Hudson, 1984.

A. Planta. "Zum römischen Weg über den Grossen St Bernhard" *Archaeologica Helvetia* 37 (1979) 15-30.

Polybius. *History*, Book III, Chapters 53-60. Also 34.10.

John Prevas. *Hannibal Crosses the Alps*. New York: Da Capo/Perseus, 1998.

David Soren, A Ben Khader and Hedi Slim. *Carthage*. New York: Simon and Schuster (1990) 160-1.

152

Konrad Spindler. *Derr Mann im Eis*. Ed. Betelsmann, 1993.

*Tabula Imperii Romani*. Mediolanum L-32 Map and Text. Roma: Union Academique Internationale, 1966, 92 & Map F-I,II.

Henri de La Tour. Atlas de Monnaies Gauloises, 1878 ed.

John Wallace, Peter Hobbs, *Atmospheric Science*, Volume 92, Second Edition: An Introductory Survey (International Geophysics), 2006.

G. Walser. *Summus Poeninus. Historia*, Heft 46 (1984).

K. D. White. *Greek and Roman Technology*, London: Thames and Hudson (1989).

F. Wiblé, ed. *Vallesia XXVII* on, *Chronique des découvertes archéologiques dans le canton du Valais*, Sion. 1980-2000.

_____."Quelques reflexions sur la 'romanisation' du Mont Joux, in Ceux qui passent et cuex qui restent, Études sur le traffics transalpins et leur impact local." *Actes du Colloque de Bourg-Saint-Pierre 1988* (1989) 191-204.

_____. "Le temple de Jupiter Poeninus, au sommet du Col du Grand-St-Bernard, érige ou reconstruit à l'époque flavienne?" *Bulletin d'Etudes prehistoriques alpines*, VII-VIII, 1996-97, 19-26.

_____. "Cols et communications: La route du col du Gd St-Bernard." *Vallis Poenina: La Valais à l'époque romaine*. Sion: Musée cantonal d'archéologie (1999).

_____. "Le traffic commercial par le Grand Saint Bernard a la époque romaine: l'apport de l'épigraphie et de quelques données archéologiques" in *Alpis Graia: Archeologie sans frontiers au col de Petit-Saint-Bernard*. Italia-Franchia ALCOTRA Projet Interreg IIIA (2006) 285-89.

Spenser Wilkinson. *Hannibal's March through the Alps*. Oxford: Clarendon Press, 1911.

R. C. L. Wilson, S. A. Drury and J. L. Chapman. *The Great Ice Age: Climate Change and Life*. Routledge, 2000.

H. E. Wright, J. E. Kutzbach, T. Webb, W. F. Ruddiman, F. A. Street-Perrott and P. J. Bartlein. *Global Climates Since the Last Glacial Maximum*. University of Minnesota Press, 1993.

# INDEX

154

orogeny, 45

Orographic, 5

Ötzi, 12, 26, 27, 93

Oxidation, 12, 14, 25, 93, 126

Paleoclimate, 4, 114, 115

Palynology, 20

Pennine Alps, 9, 20, 22, 48, 52, 53, 60, 68, 77, 79, 111

Petite-St-Bernard, 79, 104, 106

Petrography, 46, 47, 50, 53, 55

pH, 14, 17, 29-43

Phoenicians, 124-5, 130, 131-2

Plan de Barasson, 38, 72, 74, 82, 90

Plan de Jupiter, 36, 48, 51, 55, 67, 74, 82, 91, 92

Polybius, 48, 79, 98, 99, 102-6, 110-14, 118-9, 121, 123, 130-1

Prevas, J., 100, 104-5, 109, 116-8, 121, 152

Punic, 98, 111, 124-7, 129-32

Punic Wars, 126

Queyras, 24, 109, 110, 118

Rhone River, 118

Roads, 67-70, 75

Romans, 2, 27, 38, 46-8, 50, 51, 57, 60, 67-75, 77-9, 83-5, 87, 92-5, 129-130

Roman technology, 24, 25, 41-2, 59, 61-4, 73, 75, 78, 80-2, 90-1, 126

Salassi, 42, 48, 53, 74, 78-9, 87, 99, 106, 111

Savine Coche, 117, 119, 121

Savine Lac, 102

Scipio, Cornelius, 129

Sequani, 24, 78, 82-3

Soil, 12-4, 17, 23-5, 29-31, 33-41, 43, 73

*spolia*, 57-9, 61-3, 65-6

Stanford Alpine Archaeology Project, 19, 29, 33, 49, 57, 67, 73, 97-8, 106, 109, 123, 126, 133

Strabo, 48, 71, 79

Stratigraphy, 12

Summus Poeninus, 47-8, 59, 70-2, 79, 92